Irish Reporter Publications:

# EXPOSURE

## Living With Radiation In Ireland

John O'Dea

IRISH
REPORTER
PUBLICATIONS

First published in 1997 by
**Irish Reporter Publications**
PO Box 3195, Dublin 6, Ireland

**ISBN 1 - 900 900 - 01 - 7**

**Irish Reporter Series Numbers 24-25**

Layout and Design: HVis
Pictures:
Derek Speirs: Cover (Lettermacaward, County Donegal) and pages 28, 42
Courtesy of BNFL: Pages 17, 19, 21, 23,
Courtesy *of The Irish Times*: Pages 45, 46
Courtesy of the RPII: Pages 89, 100

Printed by Elo Press, Dublin

John O'Dea is a lecturer in environmental physics at
Sligo RTC. He has a long record of involvement in
social and cultural activities, including a spell as
chairperson of Sligo CND.

Born in Roscommon, he now lives in Sligo town,
with his wife, Siobhan, and children,
Sophie and Tom.

He believes that the future of the environment
depends not only on largescale governmental action,
but also on informed individuals living their lives in
a spirit of humility, respect and care for the earth.

*Dedicated to my family,*
*Siobhan, Sophie and Tom.*

# *Contents*

# *Introduction*

Although radiation has been with us since the creation of the universe, our awareness of it in a scientific sense is very recent, with our knowledge of radioactivity being only one hundred years old in 1996. In 1896 the French scientist Henri Becquerel discovered that certain substances spontaneously emitted a mysterious form of ionising radiation and a few years later the Italian, Guglielmo Marconi, was transmitting non-ionising radio waves across the Atlantic. Imagine a world without radio, telecommunications, nuclear power, X-rays, radiotherapy, sunbeds, etc. The twentieth century has been the first century of exploitation of radiation. Radiation, in particular ionising radiation, is a form of energy which commands awe and apprehension. It is constantly making news.

The range of radiation issues which have commanded news attention is highlighted throughout the text, by using press clippings from 1996, the centenary year of Becquerel's discovery and the tenth anniversary of the Chernobyl accident.

Chief among continuing areas of concern are nuclear weapons, nuclear power production and waste treatment. More recently the presence of the radioactive gas radon in our homes, the growing use of X-rays in routine health care and indeed the increased use of aviation has brought the health impact of ionising radiation to the doorstep of each and every individual. To these we must add the growing awareness of the possible impact of electromagnetic radiation, originating from the appurtenances of the technological age. Does living in an electrical environment damage our health? Are microwaves radiating from devices such as mobile phones, VDUs and ovens dangerous?

This book attempts to provide sufficient information to enable the reader to make some sense of the bewildering but fascinating world of radiation and the even more confusing range of positions and evidence that are regularly bandied about in the media, political discourse and social intercourse. The full gamut of radiation topics would require many tomes to give a totally comprehensive elucidation. This effort might be seen as an attempt to take the reader from the realm of hearsay into the first stages of a wider understanding.

It is not possible to read, or truly argue, about the impact of radiation and its health implications without some understanding of the basic scientific terms and concepts that are used. Often those who are most vehement in opposing radiation are those who least understand it. Support of, or opposition to, any issue should be grounded on knowledge. Hopefully this book will add to the persuasiveness of your chosen view.

Of its very nature, any understanding of radiation requires some effort and perseverance on the part of the reader. This is a book that can be read in sections and may need to be returned to on a few occasions.

The book contains three main sections. Section A examines the world of radioactivity, including aspects such as: nuclear power and safety; Chernobyl; what happens in Sellafield; and the behaviour of radon. Section B is a review of the nature and some of the research into non-ionising radiation, from such diverse sources as microwave ovens and telecommunications, MMDS and radar antennae, UV and power line cables. Section C is a compact overview of many of the concepts that are central to an understanding of radioactivity. This has been done without the use of equations except for Einstein's familiar one of $E = mc^2$. If you are not intimidated by a little science and a few numbers you might begin with Section C. Otherwise you can begin with Section A and refer to the Basic Reference Glossary when you meet a new, unfamiliar term, *which will usually be highlighted in italics.*

The section on Understanding Radiation and the Basic Reference Glossary are to help the non-scientific reader. But there are a few simple requirements that will help the reader to understand Section A.

A radioactive substance emits three types of radiation. These are called *alpha*, *beta* and *gamma* rays. The number of emissions every second is a measure of how radioactive the substance is. This is measured in units called *Becquerels*, (Bq). 1,000 Becquerels means that 1,000 rays are given out every second.

In science the names of the *elements*, the substances that make up our material universe, are often abbreviated. For example, the symbol for uranium is U and for carbon it is C. These *symbols* are often followed by a number that tells one the relative mass (weight) of an atom. U-235 is used in atomic bombs, while C-14 is used in radioactive dating of archaeological items. Those used in this book are listed in Appendix 1.

Every topic in science involves some use of numbers and radiation is no exception. It frequently involves very large numbers and for this reason there are a number of abbreviations that are used to save space. These are familiar to most.

1,000 can be written as $10^3$, the raised number tells you the number of zeros that follow the one. $10^6$ is a 1 with 6 zeros and is therefore one million. Sometimes prefixes are used to do the same job. Kilo (k) means a thousand, mega means a million and giga means a billion ($10^9$). For example, there are about 5 billion people, or 5 G people, living on the earth. Milli means divide by a thousand and micro ($\mu$) means divide by a million. A metre (m) can be divided into 1,000 millimetres (mm) and into a million micrometres ($\mu$m). A radio dial is tuned to a frequency of so many kilohertz (kHz) or megahertz (MHz).

The following table gives some of the other prefixes one meets on a journey through the world of radiation:

| multiplier | or | prefix | symbol | multiplier | or | prefix | symbol |
|---|---|---|---|---|---|---|---|
| 1,000 | $10^3$ | kilo | k | 1/1000 | $10^{-3}$ | milli | m |
| 1,000,000 | $10^6$ | mega | M | 1/1000000 | $10^{-6}$ | micro | $\mu$ |
| 1 Billion | $10^9$ | giga | G | 1/billion | $10^{-9}$ | nano | n |
| | $10^{12}$ | tera | T | | | | |

An olympic sprinter must run 100 metres (m) in 10 seconds (s). This is an average speed of 10 metres per second. Per (/) means that the number of metres (100) are divided by the number of seconds (10). This can be written as 10 m/s. In everyday life many quantities involve units that are divided into each other. A farmer might have 20 cows/acre. A carton of milk weighs 1 kg/litre. The area of a carpet is measured in metres squared ($m^2$) and if the area is small it might be measured centimetres squared ($cm^2$). The volume of a room is measured in cubic metres ($m^3$). A gym with a length of 20 m, a width of 10 m and a height of 5 m would have a volume of 1,000 $m^3$.

If you can follow this brief introduction to the language of the scientist the terms and concepts this book shouldn't present any major difficulty for you.

# *Milestones in Radiation History*

The modern study of electricity could be said to have began in 1780 when Charles Coulomb discovered the law of attraction and repulsion between electrical charges and the existence of electric fields. It took another century of study into electricity and magnetism before Thomas Edison opened the world's first electricity generating station in New York in 1882. In the following decade Marconi sent the first wireless telegraph transmission. In that decade also, the ionising radiations of X-rays and radioactivity were discovered, by Roentgen in 1895 and Becquerel in 1896 respectively. If the world of technology is dated from man's ability to control radiation then it is only a century old. The following chronology of a century of radiation is not exhaustive but aims at giving an overview of what is a fascinating but often controversial area of human endeavour and concern.

| | |
|---|---|
| **1894** | Tesla opens an AC electricity generating station at Niagara Falls. |
| **1895** | Roentgen discovers X-rays. |
| **1896** | Becquerel discovers radioactivity. |
| **1896** | Marconi patents wireless telegraph. |
| **1898** | Curies coin term radioactivity and isolate radium. |
| **1900** | Dorn discovers radon. |
| **1901** | Marconi sends trans Atlantic radio signals. |
| **1904** | Rutherford identifies alpha particles and introduces term half life. |
| **1912** | Radium used to make instrument dials luminous. |
| **1914** | HG Wells predicts atomic destruction of major cities. |
| **1925** | A quack radium cure-all medicine introduced in the US. |
| **1926** | Baird demonstrates first practical TV. |
| **1926** | Papers published on use of radium for cancer therapy. |
| **1927** | ESB is established. |
| **1932** | Chadwick discovers the neutron. |
| **1932** | Irish Nobel scientist Walton creates first nuclear transmutation. |
| **1935** | Development of radar in UK. |
| **1938** | Hahn and Strassman split the atom causing fission. |
| **1944** | Manhattan Project set up, under Oppenheimer, to build atom bomb. Fermi creates first sustained nuclear chain reaction in Chicago University. |
| **1945** | August 6th and 9th, bombing of Hiroshima and Nagasaki. |

**1946** Rural electrification begins in Ireland.

**1947** Electronic age begins with invention of transistor.

**1949** First USSR atom bomb detonated in Kazakhstan.

**1951** First nuclear generated electricity, Idaho, USA.

**1952** First American H-bomb and UK detonates atom bomb
in Western Australia.

**1953** Concept of absorbed dose and rad introduced.

**1955** Einstein dies.

**1956** Queen opens first UK nuclear power station in Windscale.

**1957** First US underground nuclear tests.
Fire at Windscale with I-131 releases.

**1958** US nuclear bomber catches fire at Greenham Common,
denied by the US and UK.
CND founded in Britain.

**1960** First French nuclear bomb.

**1963** Limited Test Ban Treaty signed.

**1964** China detonates an atomic bomb.

**1969** First Indian nuclear power station goes on line.

**1970** Non-Proliferation of Nuclear Weapons signed by 48 countries.

**1972** Linear model of radiation risk introduced.
CAT scans introduced.

**1973** ALARA principle of radiation protection introduced by the ICRP.

**1974** *Rasmussen Report* on nuclear safety published.
Plans for THORP commence.
Thorn in the side of the US nuclear industry, Karen Silkwood,
killed in car crash.
Radio Shack introduce first personal computers,
leading to growth of VDUs.

**1975** London Dumping Convention (LDC) introduced.

**1977** Use of plutonium pellets to provide Voyager 2 with electricity.

**1978** US cancels plans for neutron bomb that destroys life,
but not property.
First cellular phones introduced.

**1979** Accident at Three Mile Island PWR plant in Pennsylvania.
Israel allegedly detonates atom bomb off South African coast.
Protests at plans to build nuclear power plant
at Carnsore Point, County Wexford.

**1981** ICRP publishes limits for the inhalation of radon gas.

**1983**   Moratorium on sea dumping of radioactive waste.

**1985**   ICRP set 1 mSv per year as dose limit for general public.
Sinking of the Rainbow Warrior in New Zealand, by the French.

**1986**   Chernobyl reactor explodes, with at least 31 deaths
due to heat and radiation.

**1987**   Yucca mountain, Nevada, designated as geological repository
for US High Level Waste.

**1990**   US judge rules that a nuclear worker died from cancer
due to exposure to radiation.

**1992**   Use of radiation to preserve fresh fruit on sale in USA.
Germans arrest seven Czechs selling smuggled uranium pellets
from the former USSR.
Pakistan builds a PWR, supplied by China.

**1993**   Cancer cluster identified in Seascale close to Sellafield.
High suicide rates reported among Chernobyl clean up workers.
South Africa announces possession and dismantling
of nuclear weapons.

**1994**   US smelter worker receives first compensation for cancer
due to NIR exposure.

**1995**   French renew weapons testing at Moruroa,
despite international opposition.
Official inauguration of THORP at Sellafield.
Greenpeace prevents dumping of Brent Spar,
which contained Low Level (LLW) radioactive waste.
Public enquiry into the NIREX plans for a repository
at Sellafield.

**1996**   Privatisation of Nuclear Electric in the UK.
Signing of the Comprehensive Test Ban Treaty
without India or Pakistan.
Large increase in technetium-99 emissions
from Sellafield, due to THORP.

**1997**   UK government scrap Nirex plan for underground
Sellafield nuclear waste repository after objections from
community groups and the Irish Government.

# A The World of Ionising Radiation

# *Radioactivity Affects Your Health*

**"Sellafield 'link' to more Down's cases"** *Sunday Tribune*

"The discovery of a second cluster of eight Down's syndrome children in Dundalk is believed to be linked to radioactive discharges caused by a fire at Sellafield nuclear plant formerly known as Windscale, on 10 October, 1957."

**"Scepticism at Sellafield report"** *The Irish Times*

"The British government report which says it is unlikely the Sellafield nuclear plant in Cumbria caused a leukaemia cluster among children in nearby Seascale has been met with scepticism in Ireland."

Radioactivity and X-rays, which are *ionising* radiations, are dangerous to man. They deposit energy into the body which can affect the biological functions of the body's cells. At high *doses* ionising radiation can kill cells, damage organs and cause rapid death. These doses of radioactive energy are measured in *units,* called *grays* (Gy), or somewhat similar units called *sieverts* (Sv). An instantaneous absorbed dose of about 5 Gy to the whole body would kill over 50% of victims within thirty days. This is called the *lethal dose 30,50* (LD30,50). The more complicated the organism the lower the dose that is lethal. It would take doses in the order of 200 Gy to have a similar effect on shellfish and amoebas are highly resistant to radiation damage.

At high *acute* doses of greater than 1 Sv radiation sickness occurs. The intestinal lining is damaged to a point where it cannot perform its functions, leading to nausea, diarrhoea and general weakness. At higher doses (~3Sv) the immune system is damaged and cannot fight off infection and disease. Acute whole body doses of over 10 Sv leave the victim with little chance of recovery with damage to the central nervous system. It is important to realise however that it is possible to target parts of the body, as in radiation therapy, with far higher doses than one would subject the whole body to.

If the radiation dose is delivered over a longer period of time there is a greater chance of recovery. Also if a person survives a high acute dose for about 60 days his chances of recovery are high although he will have a high risk of some late effect such as cancer or leukaemia in later life.

## Hiroshima

In Hiroshima the atomic bomb, code named 'Little Boy' was fueled by uranium and had an energy equivalent of 15 kilotons of TNT. Up to 40% of a population of a quarter of a million are estimated to have died although many would have died from the force of the blast and the resulting fireball. The initial radiation from the fireball would have been delivered in the first 5 seconds and it is estimated that the dose in this time at a distance of 1 kilometre was about 2.5 Gy, less than the $LD_{30,50}$. The dose due to *fallout*, subsequent radioactive materials falling out of the atmosphere, in the most affected area, is estimated to have been of the order of 14 mGy which is of the order of the radiation background that many people are exposed to in Europe (see second section). In other words fallout from the bomb was below levels at which biological effects are observable. Initially it was expected that Hiroshima and Nagasaki would be uninhabitable for decades, which has not proved to be the case.

## Cancer

Whereas the acute effects of radiation are easily identified it is extremely difficult to tie down the effects of low doses such as one might receive from Sellafield, radon or weapons fallout. At low doses radiation can start off partially understood chains of events which can lead to cancer and *genetic* effects. This is because the effects may not be evident for many years and when they do appear its difficult to specify the causes as cancers have so many confounding origins.

Cancers have a long *latency period*. In the first decade after the Japanese atomic explosions it appeared as if leukaemia was the main effect on the survivors. Yet by the mid-sixties it was evident the cancers by far outstripped the incidence of leukaemias. We know that radiation causes cancer from studies of Japanese atomic bomb survivors (ABS), uranium miners and animal experiments.

Cancer occurs when something goes wrong with the division in animal cells. The mechanism of cancer induction is not well understood but it is connected with the replication of cells and the function of DNA, which is a complex *molecule* with a double strand structure. Ionising radiation possesses sufficient energy to break the strands. A single strand breakage or damage can be repaired by using the second strand as a template. If both strands are broken the resulting damage may be permanent and transmitted to daughter cells as mutations.

These mutations seldom seem to cause cancer but can be the first stage in what is thought to be a two step process:

(i) *Initiation:* Radiation causes mutations by double breaks in the DNA strands.

(ii) *Promotion:* The mutated, but still controlled, cell is further damaged by a chemical agent, such as tobacco smoke. This can then turn the already damaged cell into a malignant cell in which all control of cell division is lost.

This two step model would explain the long latency period which is one of the main features of cancer.

One division of radiation effects is that into *somatic,* where the individual suffers the effect of the exposure, and genetic, where one's offspring suffers the effects. Another important division is between *stochastic* and *deterministic*. The former refers to radiation effects whose probability, or chance of occurring, depends on the size of the dose (eg, cancer, leukaemia). In the latter case the severity of the effect depends on the size of the dose and will involve some minimum threshold of exposure before the effect ensues (eg, eye cataracts, sterilization).

## *Background Radiation*

Ionising radiation engenders a lot of fear and concern especially when one hears of releases from nuclear installations or high levels of radon. Much of this concern can be placed in a proper context by comparison with our exposure to ionising radiation from the sea of radiation in which we live. This radiation, called *background* radiation, has many sources, some of it man made, but most of it natural:

(i) **Cosmic** radiation that enters our atmosphere from outer space and is partially absorbed by the upper atmosphere. Because it is greater at higher altitudes it is of particular concern to those in the aviation industry. At the earth's surface the annual average dose contribution is about 250 μSv but this would be over a hundred times greater at an altitude of 10 km.

(ii) *Terrestrial* radiation has its origins in the primordial radioactive *elements* such as uranium and thorium which because of their long *half lives* still exist in the soil and rocks beneath us. These elements provide us with a gamma ray background of about 350 μSv. Radon also arises from these terrestrial elements and is the greatest single source of background radiation. Included as a terrestrial source would be the contribution of the relatively abundant radioactive *isotope*, potassium 40 (K-40).

(iii) *Internal* radiation comes from radioactive elements that exist in our bodies of which potassium-40 is the major contributor. A 70 kg person contains about 140 g of potassium, mainly in the muscle. A small fraction (0.01%) of all natural potassium (K) is radioactive and emits beta particles. This fraction, labelled K-40, has an *activity* of approximately 3,700 Becquerels (Bq), meaning that 3,700 energy carrying beta particles are emitted every second in a 70 kg human. This contributes a dose of about 200 μSv per year, which as nuclear proponents enjoy pointing out is greater than the exposure you would receive standing outside a nuclear power plant.

## "Pilots call for airlines to act on cosmic radiation"

### The Irish Times

"Airline flight crew should be categorised as nuclear industry workers because of their high altitude exposure to cosmic radiation. One flight from Dublin to New York ... causes a radiation exposure comparable to the estimated lifetime exposure of a typical Irish person to radioactive caesium deposited here following the Chernobyl nuclear accident."

Here is the approximate activity of some common or everyday items:

| Item | Activity in Becquerels |
| --- | --- |
| 1 litre of seawater | 10 Bq |
| 1 kg of coffee | 1,000 Bq |
| 1 kg of granite rock | 1,500 Bq |
| 1 kg of coal ash | 2,000 Bq |
| 1 kg of brazil nuts | 3,000 Bq |
| 1 adult person | 7,000 Bq |
| smoke detector | 30,000 Bq |
| 1 kg phosphate fertiliser | 40,000 Bq |

After the 1986 Chernobyl accident the EU placed an upper activity limit of 600 Bq from a kilogram (Bq/kg) of foodstuffs for human consumption. A year and a half later the Nuclear Energy Board (now the RPII) found 13% of mountain sheep in Ireland to have activities above this level.

An annual consumption of 30 kg of sheep meat with this level of activity would yield a dose of 250 μSv. The normal average activity of meat is, however, less than 10 Bq/kg and the dose correspondingly lower at less than 4 μSv for a similar consumption of meat.

## "Chernobyl radiation persists in Ireland" *The Irish Times*

"Ten years after the Chernobyl explosion its radioactive legacy is still with us ... No country in Europe was prepared to deal with what happened ... this was an accident that should not have happened but it did and we were not prepared for it."

## "Sellafield toxicity in Irish Sea low" *The Irish Times*

"The level of radioactive contamination from Sellafield is now so low that it should not put people off eating fish from the Irish Sea, according to the RPII."

In 1996 the Radiological Protection Institute of Ireland (RPII) reported that heavy consumers of Irish Sea fish and shellfish were typically receiving an annual dose of 2 μSv from caesium-137 originating in Sellafield. To put this dose in perspective the same consumers receive 75 times this dose from the radio-isotope polonium-210 occurring naturally in the same fish.

It is quite clear from these figures that we do live in a sea of natural radiation. To this we must add artificial sources of radiation of which medical radiation is the main contributor. The bulk of this medical radiation is due to X-rays, with a tiny contribution (~1%), from nuclear medicine such as radiotherapy. The average annual dose is around 300 μSv although not everybody is exposed. Medical radiation is an interesting example of people undergoing the risks of radiation for the benefits. The killer can also cure.

A small fraction of artificial background is due to the testing of nuclear weapons in the atmosphere in the fifties and sixties. Caesium-137 and strontium-90, both with half lives of about 30 years, were the two most significant isotopes that resulted. Since the Partial Test Ban Treaty of 1963 levels have continued to drop. In 1963 fallout contributed 7% of the background radiation whereas in the nineties it has dropped to below 1%.

In the UK the contribution of nuclear power and waste is tiny at 2 μSv per year although it would be somewhat higher for the 'critical' groups living close to these installations. Chernobyl, in spite of the huge international media interest and rightful public concern about reactor safety and environmental effects, made a similar contribution to the average Irish background.

An overall picture of the average radiation background which totals over 3 mSv per year in Ireland is shown in the following pie chart:

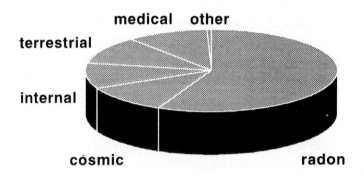

**In one hour of living in this sea of radiation we are being bombarded with about:**

  50,000 cosmic rays
  50,000 radon decays from the surrounding air
  15 million potassium decays in our diet and body
  200 million terrestrial gamma rays

**Radiation units are hard to visualise, but to get some grasp of what 1 mSv means, it is the dose we would get from:**

  4 months of exposure to radon in Ireland
  50 chest X-rays
  50 return flights to Spain
  50 years of exposure in this country of the Chernobyl radiation
  200 years of the present dose due to weapons fallout

## The Risks

The higher the dose of radiation the greater is your risk of contracting cancer, a situation that is analogous to smoking. Yet, like smoking, it is not possible to pinpoint anyone who will definitely contract radiation induced cancer, because cancer risk is a random (stochastic) process.

It is known that exposure to high doses causes a high risk of cancer. What are the risks associated with low doses and how do we go about ascertaining these risks? The International Commission for Radiation Protection (ICRP) in 1977 decided that it was possible to assume a linear relationship between dose and risk. If you are exposed to zero radiation (which is impossible) you would have zero risk of radiation induced cancer.

One can therefore draw a straight line, or linear, graph between a dose and its risk. This is called the *linear assumption* and is widely accepted by experts as being a conservative association between exposure and risk.

**A graph showing dose against risk of a stochastic effect like cancer**

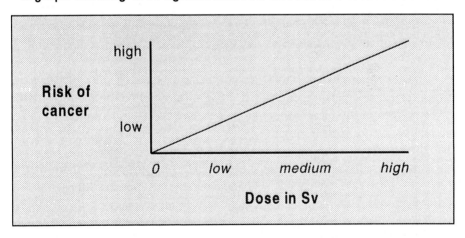

Earlier in the century it was assumed that there were threshold doses necessary to cause various effects. There are deterministic ailments, such as eye cataracts, sterilisation and skin damage (doses above 5-10 Sv), that do indeed need a certain level of threshold of exposure, but inherent in this linear assumption is that there is no safe dose that poses a zero risk of cancer or genetic effect.

## Radiation induced cancer

About 20% of deaths in Ireland annually are due to some form of cancer. This means that in any region, or medium size town of 10,000 Irish citizens, 2,000 will die from cancer. Yet we don't know **which** 2,000 will die, because it is a random process. There is therefore a very real risk that you will die of cancer in Ireland.

Evidence for the association between radiation exposure and cancer is primarily based on the studies of the atomic bomb survivors (ABS) in Japan. The risk estimates based on the ABS have limitations, such as being based on acute high dose exposure, lack of knowledge of precise doses received and ethnic differences.

The risk estimates derived by various scientific bodies have produced results that vary slightly but are still roughly in the same ball park.

In 1977 the ICRP proposed that the risk of radiation induced fatal cancer was 1 in 80 per Sv or a risk factor of 0.012 per Sv based on a life span of 70 years. Figures as high as 1 in 20 per Sv have been suggested by the National Radiological Protection Board (NRPB) in the UK. The average exposure of Irish people is about 3 mSv per year which gives a lifetime average exposure of about 200 mSv or 0.2 Sv. So, even if we use the high risk rate of 1 in 20 per Sv the risk to the average Irish person of getting radiation induced cancer would be about 1 in 100, or 1%.

If we go back to our town of 10,000 people this means that 20 of the 2,000 cancer victims run the risk that their cancer will be radiation initiated. This number would not be noticed in the larger group, given the random nature of cancer and the natural fluctuations in its occurrence.

Of course, the situation could change dramatically - for instance, if there was a severe nuclear accident in the UK, with unfavourable weather conditions from an Irish perspective. Furthermore, there are people living in houses with very high radon levels. 2-3% of the homes in this country could be providing potential radon doses of the order of 10-20 mSv yearly. Because of the linear assumption, if 3 mSv carries a risk of 1%, then 15 mSv carries a risk of 5%. This is a significant risk but it is one that can be reduced. The entire radiation background cannot be removed but in the case of radon, as with smoking, our exposure can be decreased - although unlike smoking, not eliminated.

An interesting aspect of the linear assumption is that an average dose of 5 mSv to a population of 1 million people would carry the same risk of cancer incidence as a dose of 1 mSv to a population of 5 million. In other words one would expect the same number of radiation induced fatal cancers in both groups.

It is estimated that the average dose of radiation workers in the UK is 1.1 mSv in a year over the natural background. Using the NRPB risk estimates for a working career of 45 years this gives an average risk of fatal cancer to a radiation worker of 1 in 27,000 per year. How does this risk of radiation induced cancer compare with other risks we continually encounter in our lives. The table on the next page lists the average annual risk of death in various industries and from some common causes as given by the Health and Safety Executive for the UK:

| Industry or Cause | Risk of Death per Year |
|---|---|
| all causes | 1 in 80 |
| smoking (10 a day) | 1 in 200 |
| heart attack | 1 in 300 |
| sea fishing | 1 in 500 |
| natural causes | 1 in 700 |
| coal mining | 1 in 7,000 |
| road/home accidents | 1 in 10,000 |
| construction industry | 1 in 10,000 |
| metal manufacture | 1 in 17,000 |
| radiation workers | 1 in 27,000 |
| textiles | 1 in 28,000 |

The risk of injury or death is a condition of living and many human activities imply a judgement that the benefits outweigh the related risks. Some risks, such as smoking or motor cycle racing are chosen voluntarily by individuals while others are aspects of general living such as road accidents. More rare are 'acts of God' such as lightning strikes. Usually risks of greater than 1 in 1,000 are considered unacceptable. Those in the order of 1 in 10,000 often lead to public attempts to reduce or mitigate the risks. Mitigation of elevated radon concentrations would fall into this category. Risks of below 1 in 100,000 are considered individual risks and warnings may be given, while those below 1 in a million are generally accepted without much concern. The latter could lead to 5 deaths in a year on the island of Ireland.

The nuclear industry poses threats that could have severe implications for large numbers and whole populations. Hence the importance of risks being kept sufficiently small as to be acceptable in relation to the benefits of nuclear power. Reactor safety is discussed later.

In fact the NRPB quote the actual fatality rate in the nuclear power industry as being considerably better than the average of all radiation workers at 1 in 70,000. This industry would be rated as a safe industry to be employed in. *(A 50 year dose from Chernobyl in Ireland carries a risk of 1 in 500,000 which is twice the risk of death from getting a chest X-ray)*

As a rough rule of thumb it seems that a dose of 1 mSv carries with it a yearly risk of fatal consequences of about 1 in 20,000 (to 30,000). This is a similar risk to flying about 100,000 km, bussing about 4,000 km or cycling about 600 km.

If we take 3 mSv as the average background dose on this island and that the population is 5 million then we could multiply the population by the dose and by the risk factor to find the number of people who run the risk of background radiation induced cancer. This figure is approximately 500 in a country where about 45,000 people die annually, which is fairly similar to the 1% risk mentioned above - remember risk assessments vary.

## Genetic effects

The other late stochastic effect of radiation along with cancers is hereditary damage. Here the testes and the ovaries (gonads) are the sensitive organs and radiation can cause mutations in the DNA of the sperm and the eggs. The defects can lead to death, mental retardation or other effects such as skin blemishes.

Many of these effects seem to occur spontaneously in any population but natural background radiation may make a contribution. Strange as it may seem, studies of the children of the ABS in Japan has failed to show any statistically significant increases in genetic defects over what one would expect to find in the general Japanese population. This means that the number of ABS children with genetic defects wasn't greater than the natural fluctuations that would be expected to occur in the population.

Similarly, it is difficult to say that the genetic defects exhibited by the Chernobyl Children, holidaying in Ireland, are due to the reactor accident of 1986, because of the large number of spontaneous genetic defects that exist in the Belarus or any other population. The evidence for hereditary damage comes entirely from animal experiments where large doses and fast dose rates are often used.

### "Chernobyl's walking dead" *The Irish Times*

"ten years after the worst environmental disaster in modern history, millions of children are suffering from cancer, millions of people have been displaced and live in isolated poverty."

### "Chernobyl: the fallout myth" *The Sunday Times*

"The horrors that these (Chernobyl) face are real enough but scientists are in little doubt that whatever the cause of their deformed limbs, it is not radiation ... The existing rate of 2,000 Belarus children born each year with severe birth defects matches typical rates found elsewhere in the world ..."

Caution is advised for pregnant women, especially in the most sensitive period from 8 to 15 weeks, where there is a high risk of malignancies such as mental retardation and head size abnormalities in their children. Also the risk factors for these children getting cancer is higher than in the rest of the population. For these reasons the X-raying of pregnant women should be avoided if possible and pregnant radiation workers are subject to lower dose limits than normal.

## The medical uses of ionising radiation

In spite of the risks associated with radiation exposure there are times when people willingly choose this exposure for expected medical benefits. Radiation used in medicine falls into two categories, diagnostic, mostly with X-rays and therapeutic where radiation is used to kill cancerous cells. The former dominates and contributes over 90% of the background medical dose to the population.

X-rays are so common that about half the population could have one every year while the frequency of use of nuclear therapy would only be sufficient to give less than 1 in a 100 a single exposure each year. On the other hand the individual doses received are low for X-rays (20 µSv for teeth and chest) and much larger for radiotherapy. X-rays are most often administered to the chest, limbs and teeth whereas the greatest doses received are with barium meals and barium enemas for 'seeing' soft tissues. Because the use of X-rays is so frequent it contributes significantly to the artificial background and therefore the collective dose to the population. It is important that diagnostic radiation be kept to the optimal minimum required to do the job, with proper maintenance of equipment, strict dose control and efficient shielding of sensitive organs and the operators.

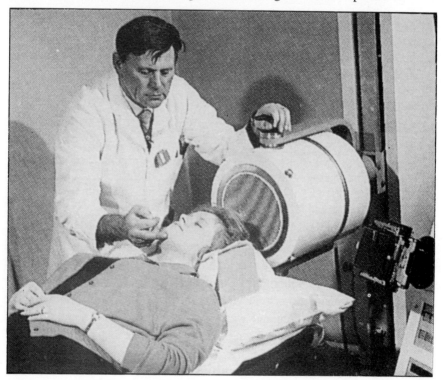

High levels of radiation can kill cells or keep them from growing and dividing and therefore radiation therapy is useful for treating cancers. Doctors limit the intensity of treatments and the amount of tissue targeted so it is the cancer that will suffer and not the 'rest' of the patient. Half of all people with cancers in the US are treated with radiation and the success rate of having radiation treatment alone or in combination with chemotherapy or surgery is rising.

Radiation therapy can be in two forms, external or internal, with some patients having both. In external therapy an instrument directs high energy rays or particles at the cancer and a margin of surrounding normal tissue. High energy X-rays or gamma rays from cobalt-60 are the most commonly used. High doses in the order of tens of grays are needed to kill malignant cells.

Whole body doses of these magnitudes would frequently be fatal so the focusing power of the machines used in radiation therapy is very important and small deviations from the target volume would have serious consequences for the patient. Since this type of treatment is usually carried out on older people the long term somatic consequences are less urgent and genetic effects irrelevant.

With internal nuclear medicine a radioactive gamma source, in sealed or unsealed form, is administered to the patient. In the former the source is sealed in a tube called an implant and placed directly into the tumour or inserted into a body cavity. An unsealed source is given as a drug injected intravenously or alternatively swallowed. The drug is chosen so that it is preferentially taken up by the malignant organ or tissue. The movement of the radioactive drug through the body can be scanned by radiation detectors. The most frequently used radionuclide in nuclear medicine is technetium-99 as it is easily generated in a hospital and it poses few waste problems as it has a short half life of 6 hours. Also, it is easily incorporated into medicines.

### "... staff are exposed to excessive radiation" *The Irish Times*

"staff who treat women for cervical cancer have to manually implant radioactive caesium in the womb .... Staff were being unnecessarily exposed because of the absence of a special remote unit ..."

In spite of the high standards of professionalism in western medicine there are still accidents and incidents that can occur in the use of ionising radiation. These include exposing the wrong patient, irradiating the wrong part of the body, administering the wrong dose and the patient being, unknowingly, pregnant. Other problems, which are shared with the industrial and educational use of radioactive materials, range from the spilling of radiopharmaceuticals to the loss of radioactive implants. Strict quality control procedures are essential for safe practice and disposal of these hazardous materials.

# The Nuclear Power Industry

We are an energy hungry age. Modern living with its sophisticated technology would be impossible without a huge supply of relatively cheap energy. Rich countries gobble the stuff up while poor countries do not have enough of it to provide a reasonable living for their citizens. An average American uses 10,000 units of energy a year compared with under 250 in India. Electrical energy accounts for about a third of all the energy used and the demand for it is expected to increase as the world's population grows exponentially to an expected 8.5 billion by 2025. Electricity is produced from fossil and nuclear fuels and also from renewables such as sun, wind and water.

The present reserves of oil and gas are expected to be depleted by the middle of the 21st century, during the lifetime of today's children, while coal resources are predicted to vanish by 2200. The loss of fossil fuels may bring environmental benefits, since the burning of them is associated with the production of large quantities of sulphur dioxide, which is associated with acid rain and

carbon dioxide, itself suspected as a major contributor to the greenhouse effect. (It is also worth noting that the burning of coal contributes nearly as much to the natural radiation background as discharges from the nuclear industry, although both doses are small, being 1 and 2 $\mu$Sv respectively). Coal has many industrial applications as in providing the raw material for plastics, dyes and so on. Why burn such a valuable resource? Furthermore, many countries have pledged to reduce their $CO_2$ emissions in the coming period.

There are many possibilities for renewable energy, such as wind and tidal power, geothermal energy, solar power and hydro-power. Of these the latter is the most practical at present and contributes about 20% of global electricity demand. All the others have various limitations and cost implications, although their attractiveness will probably improve with time as other sources diminish.

Such scenarios are the bread and butter for advocates of the nuclear power generating industry. They claim that nuclear fuel solves the dual problems of dwindling fuel supplies and pollution. Uranium (U) is plentiful and relatively cheap, and small quantities of it can generate huge amounts of power. One tonne of U is equivalent to 20,000 tonnes of coal. If *'fast breeder reactors'* were to be used (they are not at present) they could generate 60 times as much energy as a conventional reactor and create/breed fuel which would extend the use of the world's uranium supplies for more than 1,000 years.

Seeing that nuclear electricity is such a 'good thing' we should understand a little more about its operation. Firstly, it is worth noting that it is fairly popular in many countries. There are more than 400 nuclear power stations in operation in over 30 countries, worldwide. France is the most dependent on nuclear power, generating about 70% of her electricity using nuclear fuels, with Belgium not very far behind. Many of the other European countries generate between a quarter and half of their electricity this way, while the US and the UK are about 20% dependent on nuclear power.

This growth of nuclear powered electricity generation is quite remarkable, given that the first sustainable nuclear reaction only took place at the University of Chicago in 1944, under the eye of the Italian, Enrico Fermi. Less than a year later the awesome power of an uncontrolled nuclear reaction was devastatingly unleashed in Japan. It was another six years before the first electricity was generated from atomic power, in Idaho. Five years later, in 1956, Windscale opened in the UK.

To understand where all this energy comes from we must look at the splitting of the *atom*, a process called *fission*.

There are two main types of uranium isotopes: U-235 and U-238. The latter isotope accounts for over 99% of all uranium, while 0.7% of natural uranium is U-235. If you hit U-238 with a slow moving *neutron* (energy in eVs) not a lot happens, but if you do the same to U-235 the atom splits into roughly two halves, plus some free neutrons. This is called splitting the atom - or fission.

The fission products are medium sized elements like caesium (Cs), iodine (I), strontium (Sr), barium (Ba), krypton (Kr) plus a few spare neutrons etc.

The following is an example of a fission reaction (or splitting the atom):

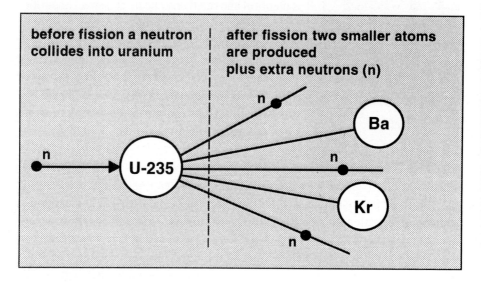

**before fission a neutron collides into uranium**

**after fission two smaller atoms are produced plus extra neutrons (n)**

This can also be written as a fission equation using the symbols for the elements where the upper number gives the atomic masses of the particles and the lower numbers give the number of protons in each particle.

$$_{92}U^{235} + {}_0n^1 = {}_{56}Ba^{141} + {}_{36}Kr^{92} + 3{}_0n^1$$

Strangely, although the masses before and after the reaction appear to add up (235 + 1 = 141 + 92 + three ones), in reality the mass of the products of the fission is always less than the mass of the U-235 atom plus the initial neutron bullet. Has the law of the conservation of matter, which states that matter cannot be created or destroyed, been broken? No, the possibility of this occurring was predicted in 1921 by Einstein when he suggested that matter (m) could be converted into energy (E) according to the equation $E = mc^2$ where c stands for the speed of light ($3.10^8$ m/s). From this equation one can, by simple multiplication, see that 1 kg of mass could be turned into an enormous amount of energy ($9.10^{16}$ Joules), sufficient to boil 200 million tonnes of cold water or almost a million cubic metres of water. The extra three neutrons produced in the above reaction can split another three U-235 atoms producing more energy, more fission fragments and 9 more neutrons.

Very quickly a large number of neutrons are available and a chain reaction can take place. All this happens in a fraction of a second and if no attempt is made to control the supply of neutrons and if there is enough uranium or plutonium (a critical mass) to intercept the neutrons a huge amount of energy is released, as in an atomic explosion.

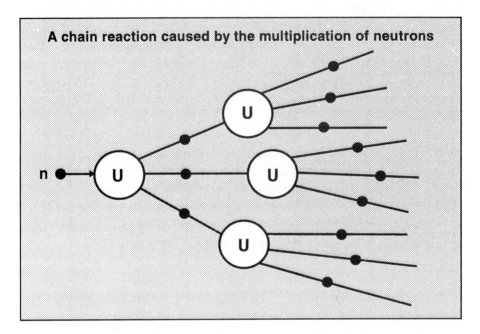

**A chain reaction caused by the multiplication of neutrons**

In a nuclear reactor the rate of fission is regulated by controlling the number of neutrons available to cause fission. Firstly, they must be slowed down, otherwise they would bounce off the U-235 isotopes and not cause fission. This is achieved by using a material called a moderator, such as graphite, in the UK's Magnox and Advanced Gas Reactors (AGR), or heavy water ($D_2O$), as in Canadian reactors, or ordinary light water ($H_2O$), as in the Pressurised Water Reactors (PWR) used in the US and elsewhere. In a reactor the number of neutrons available to cause fission is determined  by control rods which are made from materials such as cadmium which can absorb the slow moving neutrons. These are placed between the nuclear fuel elements.

To start a reaction the control rods are gradually withdrawn out of the reactor core which contains the fuel. Eventually a point is reached when one neutron from each fission goes on to produce one more fission. When this occurs the reactor is said to have gone critical.

If the control rods are withdrawn further then the number of neutrons available to cause fission multiplies and the reaction goes super-critical and too much heat will be released. The rate of the reaction is governed by the movement of the control rods. In an emergency these rods can be dropped back into the reactor core to make the reactor go sub-critical and thus stopping the reaction. *(In Chernobyl the operators were too late in dropping the control rods producing the well documented explosion)*

During the reaction the core gets very hot and this heat must be carried away, otherwise the temperature would rise to a point when the metal containing the fuel and the fuel would become molten, causing what is called a meltdown. This heat is carried away by the coolant, which in the UK reactors is the gas $CO_2$ and in the PWRs it is $H_2O$. This heat is used to turn water into steam to drive turbines and thus generators in the same way as in conventional power stations.

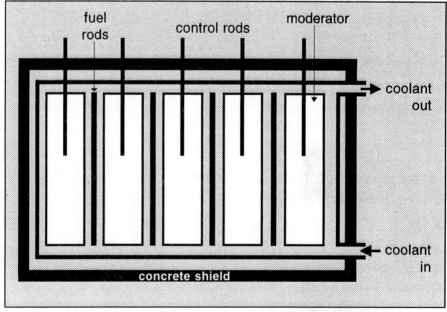

**Outline diagram of a nuclear reactor**

The fresh fuel pellets used in reactors are only mildly radioactive and can be held in the hand. After irradiation by the neutrons there is an enormous increase in radioactivity, mainly due to the creation of the fission products, with their short half lives. After a period of a couple of years in the reactor the fuel has outlived its usefulness and has to be replaced. The removed fuel is called the spent fuel. This spent fuel is very hot due to the energy of these fission products. So after the fuel is spent the residue is very hot and radioactive and must be cooled and shielded for a period of time. This is achieved by storing it in cooling ponds of water.

*A storage pond at British Nuclear Fuels*

## Reactors in the UK

**"Too close for comfort"** *The Sunday Tribune*

"... the Nuclear Installations Inspectorate referred to the 'blatant failure of Nuclear Electric's safety culture' and said that the events at Wylfa (Magnox reactor near Holyhead) were potentially the most serious in the UK during his time as chief inspector."

In spite of the greater inherent unsafety of reactors in eastern Europe the nuclear sites of greatest concern to the Irish population, in terms of potential danger, are those of the UK, due to their close proximity. Britain's electricity is generated by three types of reactors: six Magnox sites, called after the magnesium alloy cladding used to house the uranium metal fuel, seven Advanced Gas Reactor (AGR) sites, using gas as both moderator and coolant and a new Pressurised Water Reactor (PWR), at Sizewell in Suffolk. Together they total approximately 30 operating reactors. AGRs and the PWR, unlike the Magnox, use enriched uranium.

This means that the normal 0.7% U-235 that exists in uranium ore is boosted to between 2% and 4% by a process called fuel enrichment. This fuel is used in the form of a uranium oxide as opposed to the metallic Magnox form. Enriched fuels cause a more intense reaction, producing greater energy than the Magnox fuel but also producing spent fuel that is more difficult to reprocess. Fuel from the AGRs and PWRs had to await the arrival of the Thermal Oxide Reprocessing Plant (THORP) before it could be recycled at Sellafield.

In 1989, when the state run electricity system in the UK was being privatised, the government had to withdraw the nuclear component from their plans as City investors were unwilling to take on the responsibilities associated with the industry, especially the huge costs of the decommissioning that is imminent for a number of the ageing Magnox reactors.

Two new state sector companies were set up to manage nuclear reactors, Nuclear Electric for England and Scottish Nuclear for north of the border. In 1996 the privatisation took place when these utilities, minus the Magnox components, were floated on the stock exchange with many small investors taking initial losses. Prior to the flotation three of the reactors developed technical faults, but small shareholders were not informed of these problems. The new company, British Energy, is expected to realise less than half the target price hoped for by the government. Yet again public confidence in matters nuclear remains a shaky thing.

Also, as often happens, only the commercially attractive portion of an operation is made available for privatisation with the state being left with the unprofitable portion. So it is in the UK with the reactor sell off. The Magnox reactors, being older and rapidly reaching their sell by date, remain in state hands. Three are already in the initial stages of decommissioning, which will take at least 100 years.

## "Ex nuclear boss slams sell-off" *Independent on Sunday*

" A former director of BNFL has launched a scathing attack on government plans to sell off the industry, arguing that British Energy is unready and unfit for privatisation ... The government is saying: here are some reactors, working pretty well. We think we have a grip on the risks, but we're not quite sure, so we are selling them very cheaply."

## "British Energy may go for £1.3 bn" *The Times*

"The figure is half the government's target of £2.6 bn. It is also less than half what it paid to Magnox Electric, which is remaining in state hands, for the loss of the modern fleet of generators and to fund its clean-up costs of nearly £18 bn."

To complete the picture of the civilian involvement in major nuclear industry in the UK one must include British Nuclear Fuels plc (BNFL) which is involved in

almost all stages of the nuclear fuel cycle (see diagram over page), from fuel manufacture to waste storage, including the operation of two Magnox stations. From an Irish perspective it is worth noting that all their installations are close to us - being situated in the Lancashire and Cumbria region. So along with the well known Sellafield in Cumbria one could add, although they pose less of a radiological threat, the fuel manufacturing plant at Springfields near Preston, the uranium enrichment

*BNFL storage facility at Drigg*

facility at Capenhurst near Chester and BNFL's two Magnox stations at Calder Hall in Sellafield and Chapelcross across the Scottish border near Dumfries.

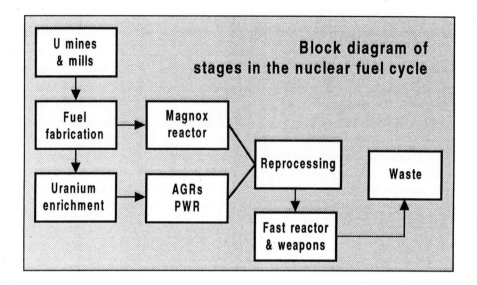

## *Nuclear Accidents*

Whereas accidents can and do happen in reactors the fuel as such is not sufficiently close together or compacted for it to produce an atomic bomb like explosion. In the case of a meltdown it is possible for the fuel to go into a critical condition and produce a nuclear explosion. In the absence of a cold war scenario, or some rogue act of nuclear terrorism, nuclear power plant accidents pose the most serious nuclear threat to the environment and human life. Reactor safety is an important issue and often the secrecy that surrounds nuclear events does little to instil public confidence.

A nuclear reactor contains a large amount of radioactive material within its central core which in a perfectly operating system, free of technical malfunction, human error or interference should pose little or no danger to anyone. If there was a major accident then large amounts of radioactive material could escape into the environment and harm plants and animals. Therefore the nuclear industry in the west takes safety very seriously. It has identified the possible things that might go wrong and has set up fail safe systems, back-up systems and multiple barrier methods to combat them.

An example of a safety feature would be that the control rods would be designed in such a way that if there was a power failure they could fall back into the reactor under the influence of gravity and thus inhibit the fission reaction. Another would be that if the core of a PWR got very hot the water moderator would turn to steam. This would constitute the loss of the moderator and through this less neutrons would be moderated and available to cause fission of the U-235. Thus the reaction would slow down.

For a large release of radioactivity to happen a series of failures would have to occur. These would include loss of coolant, overheating of fuel rods and malfunction of control rods. Then radioactive material would have to escape from the steel reactor vessel and breach the concrete containment shield. The design of nuclear structures is amongst the most exacting in the world and events as unusual as earthquakes and aircraft crashes are allowed for. In the UK station owners must show that the annual risk of accident is minuscule, in the order of 1 in a million yearly. The safety record of the nuclear industry in the Western world is good, as was seen in the risk tables for fatalities. Up to this point there has been no major accident at an electricity generating plant in the UK.

The Windscale accident of 1957 was at a military reactor as were the three deaths at a reactor in Idaho in 1961. In the US only seven fatal accidents have occurred altogether since the advent of nuclear power. Six of these were associated with military research and the last occurred in 1964, which is probably a testament to improved safety procedures as experience with reactor technology grows.

## "Deadly shadow hangs over Europe" *The Guardian*

"Ten years after Chernobyl, 27 other power reactors of the same Soviet design, or some equally dubious vintage are still threatening nuclear disaster ... Western campaign to shut them down ... has failed to secure a single closure ... Those operating the old Soviet designed reactors have learned that offers of Western help are usually contingent on profitable contracts for foreign firms ...

## Chernobyl

On Monday 28th April, 1986, technicians at a Swedish nuclear power station recorded abnormally high levels of radiation. Checks on their reactor indicated no leaks. The prevailing winds were coming from the south east and explanations were demanded from the USSR. Later that day Moscow announced that an accident had taken place two days previously at Unit 4 of the Chernobyl nuclear power plant in the Ukraine. Thus began what *Time* magazine described as by far the gravest crisis in the 32 year long history of commercial atomic power.

In the Chernobyl accident, which was caused by operator error, 3 people were killed almost immediately. About 400 people, including firemen, were involved in the initial response to the explosion. These received the highest radiation doses. About 240 people were hospitalised with severe radiation sickness and 28 of these died within weeks of the accident. Their doses ranged from 1-16 Sv. The majority of those with doses higher than 5 Sv died. Official figures claim that 31 died as a result of the accident. Ten years later most western scientists and relevant bodies appear satisfied with these figures. How many will die in the future is difficult to ascertain, particularly as information on the thousands of liquidators (workers sent in to directly clean up and make safe) who would have received significant doses is sketchy and they have been dispersed throughout the old USSR. Many groups, such as the Green Party and Greenpeace, contest the official figures.

*Workers concreting the damaged reactor*

The total radioactivity released from the Chernobyl accident is estimated to be about ten million tera Becquerels ($10^{19}$ Bq). The releases of caesium-137, the isotope that made the biggest impact on Ireland, were, strangely enough, only about 10,000 times that legally discharged from Sellafield in 1995. After the initial response to the accident over 200,000 (Greenpeace say up to 800,000) people participated in the liquidation of the consequences of the accident. These were mostly military personnel and they fought the continuing fire, built the sarcophagus that entombs Unit 4 and were involved in clean up activities. Their average dose is estimated to have been about 100 mSv while 10% received doses of the order of 250 mSv (the Irish background dose is about 3 mSv while acute doses geater than 1,000 mSv have serious health consequences). In spite of pro-nuclear organisations such as the International Atomic Energy Agency (IAEA) suggesting that the confirmed radiation induced fatalities are low, there is evidence that the health, both physical and mental, of victims, particularly that of liquidators, has sharply deteriorated, even when compared with the relatively poor health of the general ex-USSR population. Many of the liquidators would have received external doses comparable with Japanese atomic bomb survivors and similar health consequences, leukaemias, cancers and immune system damage, should be expected to occur with the passage of time.

Discussion on the consequences of Chernobyl are bedevilled by the lack of clear and agreed information on almost every aspect of the disaster, such as numbers of liquidators, numbers evacuated, dose levels, contamination of the environment and foodstuffs, etc. Health effects are hard to distinguish from those that would be expected to occur naturally in the general population. Thousands have died of cancer in the region since the accident but the number attributable to radiation from the accident is difficult to determine given the normal incidence of disease and may well be very low. There is no doubt, however, that Chernobyl was a major ecological and psychological disaster for a region that was and continues to be beset with significant problems of economic development and public health.

Large scale evacuations were put into operation in the days after the accident. Over 100,000 local people were evacuated from a 30 km exclusion zone around the power plant. Less than 10% of these are estimated to have received doses greater than 50 mSv which was the ICRP annual dose limit for radiation workers until recently.

The release of iodine 131 was larger than that of caesium but as it has a short half life of 8 days its radiological impact was short lived. However, radio-iodine was absorbed into the bloodstream by ingestion of foodstuffs, mainly contaminated milk, and by inhalation of the initial radioactive cloud. Iodine is accumulated in the thyroid, especially by children. Not surprisingly a dramatic increase in thyroid cancer has been observed in the region. The increase in thyroid cancer has been 100-fold in Belarus and hundreds of cases have been recorded in both Belarus and the Ukraine. Thyroid cancer is the most obvious and scientifically accepted health effect of the accident. Thyroid cancer is now deemed as treatable.

Significant increases in other types of health disorders in Belarus have been claimed, but again, making a definite connection with Chernobyl radiation is statistically difficult.

There are many reactors in eastern Europe that are considered to be inherently unsafe. There are a number of a similar construction to Chernobyl Unit 4. The cost of making them safe, by Western standards, will run to billions of pounds, well beyond the capacity of these countries to pay. Chernobyl has put a grave doubt over the safety of the worldwide nuclear power industry.

## The probability of an accident

Perhaps the most famous study on reactor safety is the *Rasmussen Report* published in the USA in 1975. It compared the probabilities and consequences of reactor accidents of various degrees of severity with those associated with other natural and man-made sources of risk. The risk of a fatality due to a reactor accident was many orders of magnitude less. The risk of fatality due to 100 operating reactors was given as less than one in a billion as compared with a risk of one in a thousand from all other accident sources. The *Rasmussen Report* is not without its critics.

Yet accidents and incidents do occur regularly and with varying degrees of severity and consequence. Ireland is threatened in two ways by nuclear power generation. Firstly by accidents and secondly by the continual discharge of small quantities of radioactivity from nuclear installations.

Nuclear accidents can now be graded in terms of severity by a seven point International Nuclear Event Scale. Events from 1 to 3 are termed incidents, while those from 4 to 7 are accidents:

| 7 | major accident | Chernobyl, 1986 | major release with widespread health impact |
|---|---|---|---|
| 6 | serious accident | Windscale, 1957 | significant release |
| 5 | accident with off-site effect | Three Mile Island, USA, 1979 | limited release with severe core damage |
| 4 | accident mainly in installation | Saint Laurent, France, 1980 | minor release with health effects to workers |
| 3 | serious incident | Vandellos, Spain, 1980 | on-site contamination |
| 2 | incident | numerous | potential safety consequences |
| 1 | anomaly | numerous | deviations from authorised practice |

On this scale Ireland could only suffer from 'severe' accidents at level 5, 6 and 7 as all the others are on-site events where the releases of radioactivity are minor and within prescribed guidelines. In the half century of nuclear power there have been four severe accidents, the above three plus the 1957 explosion of an underground, high level nuclear waste storage tank near Kysthym in the Urals which may have been on a scale similar to that of Chernobyl.

In 1995 there were seventeen events reported at level 1, eight at level 2 and one at level 3. In 1996 there 23 category 1 anomalies reported in Sellafield. As with all types of accidents and disasters, the greater the severity the less the likelihood of occurrence.

## "150 'incidents' at Indian nuclear plants" *The Irish Times*

"... India's nuclear power plants were among the world's least efficient and most dangerous ... India operated some of the world's most accident prone ... nuclear facilities"

The nuclear cycle can be divided into three parts: the front end - up to the reactor; the reactor itself; and the back end - spent fuel and waste. The front end is unlikely to pose a threat of severe accident because the processes do not involve high temperatures and pressures and the finished product, the fuel, is not very radiotoxic.

The processing plants have a good safety record. The reactors and the back end with their highly radiotoxic and heat producing spent fuels and wastes are obviously sources of threat.

In the event of a severe accident in the UK (or elsewhere) the threat will depend on factors such as the scale of the accident, the distance of the accident from us and the climatic conditions at the time.

The *Rasmussen Report*, using a complicated mathematical approach called Probability Risk Assessment (PRA) to estimate the frequency and the consequences of severe accidents, estimated the frequency of fuel melting (a meltdown) in PWRs at about 1 in 10,000 per year of reactor operation.

Three Mile Island (TMI) was such an accident but it happened much earlier than Rasmussen predicted although he had identified the type of accident. Such a low risk sounds comforting but there are about 100 reactors in the US which means that the odds on a similar type event in the US could be closer to once in 100 years. Perhaps the TMI accident was not too surprising. Yet the partial meltdown in TMI didn't cause any deaths. On the positive side every accident and incident leads to a re-evaluation and improvement of safety procedures.

Using similar risk assessments the estimated risk of a severe accident in the Calder Hall Magnox reactor at Sellafield, the AGR at Heysham in Lancashire and in a high level waste storage tank at Sellafield (all about 220 km from Dublin) are respectively about 1 in ten thousand, 1 in a million and 1 in ten million per year. These are risks that could be described as unlikely, improbable and highly improbable, but none the less not impossible. The former could be considered as being comparable with fatalities occuring in Ireland due to a meteor strike.

It is suggested that the radiological impact on Ireland would be less than that of Chernobyl, which was minuscule when compared with the radiation background. The main pathway to Ireland would be atmospheric rather than via the sea. No immediate deaths would be anticipated as a result. Some increase in cancers over a period of 25 years as an increase in average dose to a population will carry an increase in cancer risk. Given that the threat exists the government with the Radiological Protection Institute of Ireland (RPII) have developed an emergency response plan. This involves co-ordination between the RPII, government departments, local authorities, health boards, the army and the civil defence.

Their level of preparedness and quickness of response is an unknown. Doubts about the effectiveness of such a plan have been the subject of some controversy in the Irish press at times and Irish Greenpeace have expressed serious reservations about it.

In fairness to the nuclear power industry it should be pointed out that no part of the energy production business is danger free. There have been a number of major accidents involving coal, gas and hydroelectric dams. The closest to home was the Aberfan disaster in Wales in 1966, when almost 150 people were killed. More recently, in 1992, a gas explosion in Turkey killed about 250 people. 2,000 people died in Italy in the 1960s when a hillside collapsed into a dam.

## The pros and the cons of nuclear power

Proponents of nuclear power offer many arguments in favour including:

- it provides a response to the energy demand with an abundant and relatively inexpensive fuel supply;
- the production of less atmospheric pollutants such as $CO_2$ and $SO_2$ than fossil fuel generators;
- nuclear electricity produces smaller volumes of waste than fossil fuel generation;
- provision of a mixed energy policy that prevents over-reliance on any one source that could be problematic such as oil during the OPEC oil crisis of the seventies;
- the production of plutonium for those countries interested in nuclear weapons.

The arguments against include:

- uncertainty about reactor safety;
- the hazards associated with the transport, storage and treatment of radioactive waste;
- the possible proliferation of nuclear weapons capability;
- questions about the security of plutonium;
- doubts about how safe are the present radiological standards.

The survival of the nuclear industry, like many enterprises in modern life, will probably depend on market forces and public opinion. Opposition to its existence is overall quite muted, except in exceptional circumstances such as a major accident, or occasionally in relation to the transport of dangerous wastes. The opposition is frequently confined to small concerned groups such as Greenpeace, Friends of the Earth and CND. On the other hand the widescale growth in nuclear power generation that was predicted in the seventies and gladly embraced by many western governments has not continued.

Many factors have contributed to this, such as the stabilisation and real drop in oil prices, the TMI accident and a realisation that there are hidden and unpredictable costs associated with the industry such as waste matters and decommissioning.

Some countries, such as the US and Sweden, have called a halt to their nuclear building programmes and in the latter case the government has committed itself to discontinue nuclear electricity production by the year 2020. It is hard to imagine countries, such as France and Japan, which are largely dependent on fuel imports

## Nuclear Waste and Sellafield

### "... pass burden to countless generations" *The Irish Times*

"... there are already several tonnes of deadly plutonium in sealed tanks at Sellafield ... plutonium has a half life of 24,000 years, in other words, after this length of time it will have lost only half its radioactivity"

### "Scary secrets from inside the nuclear industry"

*Sunday Tribune*

"If the plutonium mounds (from a failure in a container in 1992 at Sellafield) had been in different positions, there would have been a criticality incident - that is, an uncontrolled chain reaction ... there would have been in other words a nuclear explosion."

Ireland, which briefly courted with the nuclear experience during the ESB's Carnsore plans in the seventies, does not gain any benefit from nuclear power. This could change if she develops an interconnector with the UK grid at some future date.

Despite gaining no benefit we do suffer some consequences from our neighbour's nuclear operations. The major impact, and the one of greatest concern to the Irish government and public, is the treatment of spent fuel in the British Nuclear Fuels plc (BNFL) complex at Sellafield in Cumbria. Outside the risk of a severe nuclear accident at Sellafield Ireland also carries the burden of the chronic discharges from the reprocessing of spent fuel.

BNFL spends a fortune on publicity to achieve public acceptability of its role in the nuclear cycle. It is involved in the storage and retreatment of reactor waste, not only from the UK, but from many foreign countries, among whom Japan looms large. It is of its nature a dangerous and 'dirty business'. Safety has to be a major concern and their 'record' is regularly emphasised in their publicity. Releases to the environment are inevitable and some are officially allowed. One of the problems of having regulations for emmissions is that industry is permitted to legally pollute up to the regulatory limits. The Irish Sea is frequently referred to as the most radioactive in the world, due to Sellafield discharges, most of which are licenced.

The environmental record of BNFL is not without blemish and there is a catalogue of accidents and incidents of which the scale 6 Windscale fire of 1957 was the most serious. Full details of the extent of the radioactive releases were suppressed for three decades.

Among the catalogue of events are:

- 1973  Use of a reprocessing building had to be discontinued due to severe contamination.
- 1983  Accidental release of radioactive slick into Irish Sea. People warned not to use Cumbrian beaches.
- 1986  Half ton of uranium released into Irish Sea after nuclear dump caused increase in atmospheric radiation.
- 1989  Leak of excess nuclear waste into Irish Sea due to instrument failure.
- 1992  Leak of 30 litres of liquid plutonium caused temporary closure of plant

In the 1950s and 1960s the oceans were seen as a dump with infinite powers of dilution and the discharges of the Magnox wastes that began in the fifties were not seen as problematic. By the 1970s attitudes were changing and the 1972 UN Conference on the Human Environment in Stockholm led to the establishment of the London Dumping Convention in 1973 which set limits to the dumping of toxic wastes in the oceans. In the same year Sellafield had a problem with the corrosion of the metal cans containing the spent fuel rods while they were being stored under water. Radioactivity leaked through the corroded cans and when the cooling pond water was discharged into the Irish Sea it lead to a sharp increase in radioactivity levels, mainly radiocaesium. This awakened an Irish consciousness of the impact of Sellafield operations on this country and that awareness has grown ever since.

Improved operating procedures and technologies have caused a continual reduction of levels of radioactivity in the Irish Sea ever since, although such reductions have done little to ease the fears of the Irish public. Discharges of caesium-137 have dropped from over 5,000 TBq ($10^{15}$ Bq) in 1975 to less than 20 TBq in 1994. Annual doses to heavy consumers of fish landed in the north eastern ports of Ireland such as Carlingford have dropped from 140 µSv in 1976 to about 2 µSv in 1995. This is less than one thousandth of the natural background.

Given the questionable record of the nuclear industry in coming 'clean' on information we are fortunate in Ireland that, unlike in the 1960s, we can now independently monitor the levels of radioactivity in the seas and air around our country. Bodies such as the RPII and some of the third level institutions have the radiation detectors required. Continued monitoring is presently important because with the coming on stream of THORP the discharge mix to the Irish Sea will change somewhat.

## Reprocessing and disposal

What goes on at Sellafield? Its original purpose, that of Windscale as it was then known, was the production of plutonium (Pu) for the manufacture of nuclear weapons. It is now in the business of reprocessing spent fuel from world-wide reactors which is, or should be, a financially lucrative trade. Typically spent fuel contains 96% unused uranium, 3% highly active fission products like caesium and strontium and 1% plutonium.

Reprocessing is a chemical process which separates out these three components. The uranium can be recycled back into the uranium cycle and reused in reactors, the plutonium could be used in fast reactors if there were any or could be diverted into weapons construction. The fission products, although containing valuable metals, are too *hot* to handle and are stored awaiting eventual disposal. In an attempt to reduce the mounting stockpile of plutonium, BNFL now mixes a proportion of the plutonium with uranium to produce a reactor fuel called mixed oxide fuel (MOX).

The alternative to reprocessing is dry storage of the spent fuel until such a time as it can be safely disposed of. This type of storage could happen at the nuclear power plant rather than being transported to a central location such as Sellafield.

Because uranium is such a concentrated source of energy the actual volumes of radioactive wastes that it produces are small, when compared with other, non-radioactive industrial, and indeed with everyday domestic sources of waste. Radioactive wastes are divided into three main categories:

**(i) High Level Waste-HLW:** This is waste, mainly the fission products of nuclear reactions, which is extremely radioactive and extremely hot. It must be isolated and cooled. The quantity produced annually in the UK is small, a few cubic metres (m³) which wouldn't fill an ordinary bus. This liquid waste is stored in special double walled stainless steel tanks that are continually cooled and stored in concrete vaults in Sellafield. BNFL now have a vitrification plant where this HLW is evaporated into a dry powder and is then mixed with chemically stable glass making materials and enclosed in metal containers. These still must be stored and air cooled for decades before any permanent disposal can be considered. When the public talk of reprocessing waste they usually have HLW in mind.

**(ii) Low Level Waste-LLW:** Is contaminated waste, where the activity is below certain prescribed limits and there is no problem with heat. Included would be items such as paper towels, clothing and laboratory equipment. It is also produced in hospitals and certain industries. Low level liquid waste would include water from cooling ponds for spent fuel after it has passed through treatment plants to reduce its radioactive content. This water is then discharged to the Irish Sea through the famous/infamous 1.5 km pipe. Solid LLW from Sellafield goes to the landfill site at Drigg, a short train journey south of Sellafield.

There are difficulties with the definition of LLW, because at the lower end it can be disposed of in authorised local authority landfill sites. Anything that is remotely in contact with radioactivity can be considered LLW which means valuable space in a specialised site such as Drigg can be wasted. While LLW is low in activity the quantities are very large. Over 90% of the Sellafield waste is LLW. It is estimated that there will be over 500,000 m³ by the year 2000 and that Drigg will be full early in the next century.

On the road outside Drigg geiger counters only register background levels and one could quite safely take a walk across the site. There is, however, some concern over the water contamination that results. Whereas some countries consider containment (by geological means) the UK frequently opts for the dilute and disperse means of pollution management. More recently better landfill management practices with the use of concrete trenches have been introduced. *Leachate* from the Drigg trenches is continually monitored and is now routed directly into the Irish Sea via a pipeline rather than the local Drigg stream. This radioactivity still contributes very little to the background radiation dose. The main radio-isotope disposed of in Ireland is technetium-99 which is used in medical nuclear therapy. It belongs to the lowest (of four) categories of radiotoxiticy and has a short half life of 6 hours. It therefore poses a minimal radiological hazard to the public and has often been disposed of through the sewers.

**(iii) Intermediate Level Waste (ILW):** Includes all wastes that have activity greater than LLW and less than HLW. In Sellafield it consists of materials such as the fuel element cladding that is peeled off before the fuel is chemically reprocessed and sludges resulting from various treatments such as reducing the quantity of radioactive isotopes in cooling pond water. This waste is encapsulated in concrete inside steel drums and stored at Sellafield.

Nirex, a company owned by the nuclear industry, was set up to dispose of ILW and LLW. They tried to create an underground repository at Sellafield for the containment of these wastes. This repository was to be located 500 metres under ground and close to the Irish Sea coastline. Nirex was working on the principle of multi-barrier containment between the waste and the biosphere, particularly from ground water that could become a pathway back to the human food chain.

The barriers proposed included:

- waste in solid form
- encapsulation in cement
- steel drums
- backfill around the drums
- burial in a half mile deep rock

Nirex must show that such an option is safe and that the risk of radioactivity getting into the biosphere over thousands of years is acceptable. To do this they need to investigate the geology and hydrogeology at their chosen site, Sellafield included. To date their information comes from boreholes but they will still have to build a rock characterisation facility - a 'rock lab' - deep under ground.

Objectors to the Nirex plan opposed their undue haste in seeking a rock lab at Sellafield. It was suggested that there are far more suitable geologies than Sellafield and that this choice was based on political and economic considerations rather than proper investigation for the optimal geological site. It would be the cheapest site, because Sellafield stores the bulk of the UK's radioactive waste and less public outcry was anticipated, given an acceptance of the nuclear industry locally.

Leaked evidence from Nirex scientists suggests that the Sellafield geology might not be sufficiently impermeable to prevent radioactive contamination of water and thus a potential pathway to the human food chain. It is also felt that the cost of a rock lab, about £200 million, will mean that there would be no going back and that the rock lab is a Trojan horse to enable construction of the repository.

In 1997 the Nirex plan for Sellafield was rejected by the British government. Nirex will therefore have to seek an alternative UK site. This decision is a major setback for the nuclear repocessing industry, as it will delay a 'solution' for the disposal of ILW from Sellafield. It now also has major transport implications.

Britain is not alone in its plans for an ILW repository. The Swedes already operate one and other countries have plans in progress. The US has designated Yucca Mountain in Nevada as a candidate for a HLW repository.

## "Government case against UK nuclear waste" *The Irish Times*

"... the potential transboundary effects of such a development (the Nirex underground repository) so near to the Irish coast and centres of population ... would represent a totally unacceptable intrusion into the health, environmental and economic well-being of the Irish people"

Despite the dirty reputation of BNFL, its impact on the natural radiation background is relatively small. Routes to the biosphere by which radioactivity can reach man, be it by inhalation, ingestion or direct irradiation are called *pathways*.

Groups who are most in danger of exposure are called critical groups. It is assumed that if the critical groups receive doses that are 'safe' then the rest of the population is in no danger. There are a number of well defined critical groups associated with Sellafield.

The exposure of critical groups in the vicinity of Sellafield is via three routes:

- high consumption of seafood
- external radiation as from walks on the beach
- inhalation of airborn radioactivity

The doses received by these most exposed groups are less than 200 μSv or less than 10% of the average United Kingdom background. Doses received from Drigg are negligible.

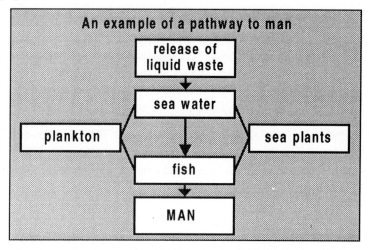

**An example of a pathway to man**

## "Can THORP be stopped" *The Irish Times*

"Economically THORP is producing a product that no-one needs and, morally, one which more and more countries do not want...German utilities have decided it is cheaper to store spent nuclear fuel in Germany than to reprocess it (at THORP or in France)."

## "Nuclear dustbin in crisis" *The Guardian*

"The plant was long ago labelled a white elephant because its original purpose-to produce plutonium for the now abandoned European fast breeder reactor program-has disappeared."

Up to the mid-nineties Sellafield could only reprocess the metallic non-enriched Magnox fuel. The newer generation reactors such as the AGRs and the PWRs use a U-235 enriched uranium oxide fuel. Their nuclear reactions are more intense given the enrichment and as a result the spent fuel is hotter, more active and contains more *transuranic* isotopes. BNFL the state owned company set up in

1971 saw the commercial opportunity in reprocessing the spent fuel from these reactors in the UK and also on a world wide basis. It sought permission to build THORP and received it after a 3 month public enquiry in 1978. It was to cost about £3 billion before going into operation in 1994. With hindsight many would question the wisdom of building THORP, but in the oil starved seventies there were a number of arguments in its favour:

**(i) Recycling uranium:** With the expected rise in oil prices and the predicted growth in nuclear power generation the price of uranium was expected to become very expensive. Therefore the recycling of uranium seemed to make economic sense. After TMI and Chernobyl and a stop to the growth of nuclear power uranium has become cheap and plentiful. Dry storage of the spent fuel is cheaper than reprocessing.

**(ii) Plutonium is valuable:** At the time much was expected from the development of fast breeder reactors (FBR) that would require plutonium as a fuel and then be able to generate more plutonium than it consumed. FBRs have never become commercial and most countries have abandoned their development. The prototype FBR at Dounreay, in the north of Scotland, was shut down in 1994.

**(iii) Waste was manageable:** At the time there was greater optimism about man's ability to manage radioactive wastes and that reprocessing was a useful means of doing this. This is no longer the case and dry storage of spent fuel is considered by many to be safer and cheaper.

**(iv) Reprocessing makes fuel safer:** Because the spent fuel is broken into fractions some of it can be used again. However one could argue that Sellafield in fact disperses the radioactivity that could have been contained in one store at the reactor site after use. It destroys none of the radioactivity but some of it goes into the Irish Sea, some into Drigg, etc. Furthermore unlike reprocessing dry storage would guarantee that the plutonium is in a condition that would prevent robbery and proliferation as it would be mixed with the dangerous fission products.

**(v) Employment:** BNFL is one of the major employers in the otherwise under industrialised county of Cumbria.

The UK authorities have had to revise their sea discharge limits - upwards - to provide for the operation of THORP. As THORP had not yet reached its full operating capacity in 1996 the RPII has had to estimate what the doses to heavy Irish fish consumers on the north eastern seaboard would be if THORP discharges were at the maximum allowed limits.

The dose would be about 12 µSv as compared with less than 2 µSv in 1995, about 5 µSv in 1991 and about 150 µSv in 1976 when discharges were at a maximum. There are recent reports of a dramatic increase in the uptake of technetium-99 in shellfish caught off the Sellafield coast, including a hundred-fold increase in lobsters to concentrations far in excess of any EU limits. Already an increase in technetium-99, in seaweed collected off Ireland, has been recorded by the RPII. Atmospheric discharges will also increase, with THORP coming onstream, particularly krypton-85, which is not very radiotoxic. Yet even if atmospheric discharges are at the maximum allowed the aerial dose will be less than 1 µSv. *(The Irish background is 3 mSv or 3,000 µSv)*

At the end of 1996 BNFL applied for a change in its discharge limits. They wish to increase aerial discharges, mainly of the radioactive H-3 isotope, tritium, while reducing its liquid discharge of technetium-99. According to the RPII such a change could cause a 20% increase in the dose of those most effected, the Cumbrian critical groups, but the increase would almost be undetected in Ireland due to dilution and dispersal in the atmosphere.

### Battles rage as nuclear cargo arrives" *The Independent*

" A 40 tonne shipment of French processed atomic waste reached a German storage depot after pitched battles between an army of riot clad police and about 3000 anti-nuclear protesters".

Ireland gains no advantage from THORP or any Sellafield activity but it does have to bear some of the risks associated with it even if these risks are small and the doses delivered are minimal. The proximity of Sellafield means that dangerous cargo ships are frequently travelling close to our shores. There is always the risk of a severe accident and the accumulation of plutonium is always a cause for concern in a world that cannot even agree on the Comprehensive Test Ban Treaty (CTBT). There is still a chance that Britain's underground repository, which will contain radioactive waste for thousands of years, might be sited just across the Irish Sea.

In this regard the initiative of the Stop THORP Alliance Dundalk (STAD) should be noted. STAD is a support group for the four people who are suing BNFL on the grounds that THORP failed to comply with EU law, as an environmental impact assessment was not carried out before the UK government granted an operating licence. This case will test the rights of citizens of one member state of the EU to object to the perceived unacceptable actions of another.

## Nuclear Weapons

### "Nuclear test ban negotiations fail" *The Guardian*

... bargaining has been stalled by India's demand that the treaty should contain a timetable for nuclear disarmament ... we want a genuine commitment to eliminate nuclear weapons within a finite time frame."

### "Yeltsin hints at nuclear concessions" *Financial Times*

"... Russia would be prepared to accept wider international scrutiny of its nuclear facilities and encourage greater co-operation between all eight countries' security services to prevent the smuggling of nuclear materials ... the condition of Russia's vast nuclear arsenal has caused increasing alarm around the world - especially following a spate of smuggling incidents since 1993."

### "Nightmare scenario: terrorists with a nuclear weapon"
*Independent on Sunday*

"... the collapse of the Soviet Union may have ended the cold war, but it has drastically increased the danger of nuclear materials, civil or military, falling into the wrong hands ... the past four years have seen no fewer than 1000 documented claims that such materials were being secretly smuggled and sold ... Even if a terrorist group was unable to provoke an explosive nuclear reaction it might using conventional explosives spread plutonium over a wide area of a city."

The greatest threat to our existence from the power of the nucleus is without doubt the huge stockpile of weapons held by the major nuclear powers: the USA, UK, China, Russia and France and the threshold nuclear powers of Israel, India, Pakistan and South Africa. To this one can add those countries that have nuclear ambitions and might be actively working on the materials needed for a nuclear weapons capability, as well as advanced nations who could quickly acquire one.

Between them they could create over 300,000 Hiroshima explosions. There are over 16,000 nuclear warheads, mainly in the hands of the US and Russia, that can be delivered to any part of the earth, with another 10,000 short range warheads.

Attempts to limit and indeed to reverse their growth have at best been half hearted. In 1959 Ireland proposed a resolution to the newly set up disarmament committee of the UN. In what became known as the Irish Resolution, they requested that an increase in the number of states possessing nuclear weapons be averted and that an international agreement be sought. After nine years of deliberation the Nuclear Non Proliferation Treaty was signed in 1968.

A partial test ban treaty, ending atmospheric and underwater testing, was signed by the USA, UK and USSR in 1963. Yet as late as 1996 the French and Chinese were still carrying out underground explosions despite huge international opposition. The need for the advanced western powers to use tests is no longer necessary - due to the development of sophisticated computer simulation technology.

At the start of the Comprehensive Test Ban Treaty (CTBT) talks in 1994 it seemed that the issue of verification and on-site inspection would pose a major problem, especially for the Chinese, but by August 1996 when the treaty was due for ratification the Indians refused to sign. They are concerned about any advantage that their traditional enemies, China and Pakistan, may have. They suggested an alternative treaty that would require the disarmament of all nuclear weapons by 2020. Such an agreement would seem to be what all sane people should aim for, but the US and indeed the other nuclear powers see such a wish as utopian.

It is not clear that a CTBT would make the world any safer although acceptance of the principle of on-site inspection suggests a major advance in international understanding. Disarmament should be the goal of the international community. Ireland is a small player in such matters, but given our position of being a 'bit' neutral, 'pretty much' unaligned and a 'bit' in Europe perhaps the Irish public should pressurise its government to keep such matters to the forefront of its international agenda. With our closer integration into a Europe that possesses nuclear weapons will we be seen as a nuclear power by association? In the post cold-war era we have become unbelievably smug about what should be the real nuclear issue. More countries now possess nuclear weapons capability than ever before, but the question of nuclear disarmament has receded as a campaigning necessity. Has it become an issue with a short half life? We ignore the ban at our peril.

# *Radon in Buildings*

## "Radon study fuels debate about risk from cancer"

*The Irish Times*

"Because radon is a gas it can be breathed in. If the radon breaks down while in the lungs it can cause tissue damage that can lead to lung cancers ... There are about 1500 lung cancers in the Republic each year and 15 to 20 per cent of these can be attributed to radon ..."

Besides nuclear catastrophes there is one area of radioactivity that poses a continual and ever present hazard and that is the radioactive radon that seeps into our homes and workplaces. But it is a hazard we have some control over, in terms of diminishing our exposure.

Radon is a radioactive gas that emanates from the ground. Uranium is present in rocks and soils in varying amounts. The average concentration of uranium in light granites is 4-6 parts per million (ppm) while in limestone it is lower at 1-2 ppm. Radon-222 is a daughter of the U-238 *decay series* (See Page 97) and its immediate *parent* is radium. There are other isotopes of radon but their impact on human exposure is much less than that of radon-222. One has a half life of 55 seconds so most of it has decayed before it can gain entry into homes. When the immediate parent, Ra-226, fires out its alpha particle the resulting radon atom may find itself pushed out of a rock or soil grain and free to migrate upwards to the surface. The more fractured the rocks and the drier the soil the easier it is for the gas to diffuse to the surface.

Concentrations of radon in the open air are low - about 10 Bq/m$^3$ - but it can gain entry into houses mainly by moving through openings and cracks in the floors. Gases move from regions of high pressure to low pressure and the inside of houses, especially in winter when heating is being used, are always at a lower pressure than outside or underneath. Once inside a building the concentration of radon builds up, especially in modern well insulated and air tight houses. Increasing ventilation can sometimes reduce the radon concentration, but perversely it can occasionally increase the suction power of the house and increase the levels. Other means of mitigation are required. The good news is that generally houses with high radon levels can have that radon successfully mitigated at reasonable cost. It is the one type of radiation you have some control over.

## Detecting radon

Radon is a very elusive visitor. Just as one would expect increased ventilation to aid mitigation you might expect houses built on granite to have higher levels of radon than ones built on limestone but there is no relationship here either. It is very hard to predict the levels of radon in a house based entirely on factors such as geographical cum geological location, types of bulding materials, rates of ventilation, degree of insulation, etc. To know the radon concentration in a particular house it must be measured. In the USA radon has become such a health issue that many house buyers expect a radon measurement to be carried out before purchase.

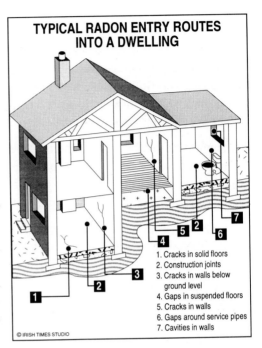

**TYPICAL RADON ENTRY ROUTES INTO A DWELLING**

1. Cracks in solid floors
2. Construction joints
3. Cracks in walls below ground level
4. Gaps in suspended floors
5. Cracks in walls
6. Gaps around service pipes
7. Cavities in walls

© IRISH TIMES STUDIO

Although there are many radon detectors they can be divided into short term and long term and both have their merits and limitations. Common short term detectors are the 'charcoal cannister' and 'the electret' which can give a radon reading after a few days of exposure. While they are common in the US they are less so in Europe. The short term test is useful if you want a quick survey on a house but as radon levels vary daily and seasonally they do not give accurate results but can still give a useful indication of a potential problem. If the test yields a high reading a follow up long term test is recommended to obtain a more realistic value.

For a more satisfactory picture a long term test is required. These can vary from three months up to a year with the latter being advisable. 'Alpha track detectors' (ATD) and long term electrets are the most popular. ATDs are made from a plastic sheet measuring 1 square centimetre that is sensitive to the alpha particles emitted by radon when it decays. The alpha particles that hit the track damage the plastic and when the detector is etched with a chemical pits appear where the alpha damage has occurred. These are visible under a microscope and can be counted to give a reading of the radon concentration. The RPII provide a cheap ATD service (£15).

## Exposure to radon

We have already seen that radon contributes the bulk of our radiation background exposing us to an average annual dose of about 2 to 3 mSv. Studies by the RPII suggest that the average concentration of this radioactive gas in Irish homes is about 60 to 80 Bq per cubic metre (Bq/m³). This means that in a volume of one cubic metre (1m x1m x1m) of air in the average Irish house that there are 60 to 80 alpha decays due to radon every second or about 250,000 decays per m³ in an hour.

A significant number of Irish homes have much higher levels and homes with concentrations of over 1,000 Bq/m³ are not uncommon. Indeed, Salthill in Galway has gained dubious notoriety for being a radon *hot spot* with some houses having even higher radon concentrations than this.

Living in a radon environment with a concentration of about 40 Bq/m³ is considered equivalent to receiving a dose of about 1 millisievert (mSv). Given the average Irish exposure to radon one can see how it contributes over half of the total background dose of 3 mSv.

In Ireland and most of Europe new houses with a radon concentration above 200 Bq/m³ are considered in need of mitigation or remedial action. Nationally over 4% of the housing stock could have radon levels greater than this 200 Bq/m³ action level, while over 10% of the houses in parts of the west of Ireland would have radon concentrations above this value. Whereas initial radon surveys in Ireland found that the west coast counties appeared to have the highest radon concentrations, recent RPII findings suggest that radon hot spots also exist in eastern counties, like Louth and Wicklow.

Because people spend less time in workplaces than in their homes the ICRP suggest that the action level for intervention in the workplace should be between 500 and 1,500 Bq/m³. In the UK there are regulations that require compliance at action levels of 400 and more stringent ones at 1,000 Bq/m³. The Department of Education in Ireland have engaged in remedial action in schools with high levels, with the aim of reducing them to below 150 Bq/m³.

# Radon risks

We know that radiation carries the risk of causing cancer and we know from the studies of uranium miners who are exposed to high concentrations of radon gas that lung cancer can ensue. The Environmental Protection Agency (EPA) in the US has identified radon as a definite carcinogen and the second leading cause of lung cancer after smoking.

The EPA in the US estimate that deaths from radon are somewhere between 7,000 and 30,000 a year. When one compares this with figures such as the 23,000 deaths from drink driving, 4,400 from fires and 1,000 from air crashes, it is clear that the radon risk should be one of genuine concern. Recent Swedish research has compared the incidence of lung cancer in people exposed over a long period to high levels of residential radon, with others in the general population.

This work lends support to the association between residential radon exposure and lung cancer. At low radon concentrations, it is not clear whether radon is a significant threat to health. Looking for connections at these exposures is probably clouded by the high incidence of lung cancer associated with smoking.

It is worth noting that while radon and smoking carry separate risks of causing cancer the combination appears to greatly increases the risks. According to the EPA in the USA, if 1,000 people who smoked were exposed to the action level of 200 Bq/m$^3$, then about 40 of them could get lung cancer, compared with 2 to 3 non-smokers with the same radon exposure. The relationship between radon and smoking seems to be synergistic rather than just additive.

It is the radon daughters that do the damage. Radon gas has a half life of almost 4 days which means that most of the radon you breathe will be exhaled before it can release many alpha particles. Its radioactive daughters, however, are solids and two of them, the two poloniums (Po), are radiologically important because they have very short half lives and are alpha emitters. Furthermore they can attach them-selves to tiny particles in the air and then be breathed in. Most of the radon dose received is due to these daughters. With their short half lives, if they get into the lung, they will deposit their alpha energy in the sensitive lining of the bronchi. These radon daughters are 500 times more likely to cause cellular damage than the parent, radon itself.

There are around 1,500 lung cancer deaths in Ireland annually. Studies suggest that 5 - 10% (some say up to 20% depending on radon exposure) of all lung cancers may be caused by radon including its decay products. We saw earlier that about 500 people might be expected to die from radiation induced cancer in Ireland due to background exposure. Over half of these could be expected to result from radon induced lung cancer. There are uncertainties surrounding all these figures as they are based on the assumption that there is a linear relationship between size of dose and the risk of cancer and one cannot be sure that this relationship applies when the doses are low.

It is not possible to pinpoint anyone who has suffered lung cancer due to radon as one lung cancer is indistinguishable from the next and may be due to other confounding factors, such as smoking or air pollution. Also it is difficult to ascertain the effect of radon using *epidemiological* studies because the radon doses to large numbers would be difficult to measure accurately, there is no form of lung cancer specific to radon and unlike smoking it is impossible to obtain a radon free control group for the purposes of comparison.

Radon exposure is usually associated with concerns about lung cancer incidence. Now certain studies are investigating possible links with other forms of cancer. Leukaemia, a disease of the bone marrow, has long been associated with high radiation doses such as with the ABS in Japan. There are now suggestions of a possible link between leukaemia and domestic radon. Possible routes to the bone marrow have been identified and corresponding doses calculated. The average UK radon exposure of 20 Bq/m$^3$ could yield an annual dose to the red bone marrow of 120 µSv. It is suggested that between 6% and 12% of leukaemia incidence could be linked to this level of exposure.

Melanoma is linked to UV exposure and in spite of its increasing incidence there are a number of anomalies - such as the high Scandinavian incidence and that UK indoor workers have a higher incidence compared with outdoor workers. The sensitive cells for cancer induction are found about 50 mm below the skin surface - which is well within the range of alpha particles from radon. A connection between this and melanoma has not been extensively studied but the possibility of radon radiation acting as an initiator, with UV as a promoter has been suggested.

Another suggestion that received a lot of publicity early in 1996 was a proposal by scientists from Bristol University of a possible link between radon levels and electric fields created by electric appliances in the home and by nearby overhead electricity transmission lines.

The suggestion is that the solid daughters of radon which often attach to dust particles in the air are attracted by the electrical forces (fields) close to electricity carrying wires and therefore accumulate close to such wires. This could be good news as the electric fields act to mop up these particles. The indoor fields of domestic appliances are too small, however, to have any significant effect on the indoor radon concentrations.

The research does suggest that the greatest concern would be the accumulation of radon daughters under outdoor high tension power lines - around which the particles would be attracted and held. The idea has been rejected by many experts including the NRPB in the UK. The reason that this research paper received so much attention is that for a number of years there has been a growing concern that there may be a connection between cancer induction and the electric and magnetic fields associated with electricity power lines and this paper suggested a possible mechanism - albeit related to ionising radon and its daughters.

As we shall see later, there are a wide range of technologies and appliances - and indeed our sun - that give out non-ionising radiation, whose possible health effects are the subject of much controversy.

## Reducing exposure to radon

It is impossible to prevent radon getting into your house because outdoor air also contains it but as most of it comes through the floor there are actions that will reduce its entry of which three are:

♦ **Sealing gas entry points:** This seems to be the most obvious solution and it could be done with some type of polymeric material, for instance PVC, but this is quite difficult to achieve in an existing house. When building a new house, however, it is both possible and inexpensive to put in place a radon proof barrier underneath the floor. New houses in radon 'affected' areas of the UK, where 10% of houses are above the 200 Bq/m$^3$ action level, must now make such a primary protection measure.

• **Pressurisation:** Most radon enters because of the pressure difference between inside and under the house. The less this pressure differential the less radon that will enter. This effect could be achieved by using internal air fans to suck in more air into the house, thus increasing the internal air pressure (the more air the more pressure just as with a car tyre). This approach which would be fairly unintrusive could cause increases in condensation and could be easily negated by normal ventilation practices, such as leaving windows open.

• **Depressurisation:** The most common way of trying to reduce radon in Irish homes is to try and eliminate the pressure difference between the inside and underneath of a house. This can be achieved by drawing air out from under the floor of the house (a secondary protection measure). A collection chamber or sump is made under the house and radon and other gases can be drawn out through a pipe by an external fan. Builders of new houses would, along with the above mentioned primary precaution, be well advised to incorporate a sump or two, plus the pipes during construction when it would cost almost nothing. If subsequent testing revealed a radon problem then a pump could easily be added. Sumps can also be placed under existing houses, but this is more difficult as one must drill at pavement level in under the flooring of the house. The cost varies but could be of the order of £500-£1,500 per sump.

In the US agencies such as the EPA have carried out cost-benefit analyses on the value of averting early death due to various risks such as road and air safety. Radon mitigation programs compare favourably. Given that modern governments seem to pay such credence to the dictums of economists maybe a strong case can be made for grant aiding radon remediation of homes. In Sweden, when the levels are greater than 400 Bq/m$^3$, home owners are eligible for a grant to cover half the cost of remediation.

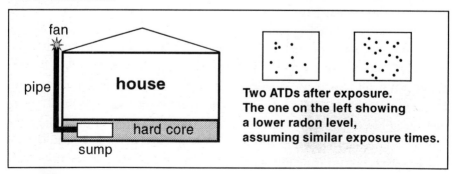

Two ATDs after exposure.
The one on the left showing
a lower radon level,
assuming similar exposure times.

# B The World of Non-Ionising Radiation

The World of Non-Ionising Radiation

## *The Electromagnetic Spectrum*

There are two main ways of delivering energy or information between two points or people. If we take a communications example we could send a letter in which case the message would be carried on a piece of matter (paper). Alternatively we could phone someone in which case our messages would be carried down a channel such as a telephone wire, a fibre optic link or though space as a radio or microwave link. The former could be described as a particular means of transport while the latter is carried on by waves or radiation. The former would be like throwing a stone at a toy boat to move it on a pond while with the latter you could try to rock the boat by causing ripples or waves on the pond. One could say that in one case the message is on the medium while in the other the message passes through the medium. Energy can be carried by particles, like alpha particles, or it can be carried by waves, like X-rays.

Waves are familiar to us all from trips to the sea or tossing stones into ponds. The distance between the crests or troughs of the waves is called the *wavelength* ($\lambda$). At the sea this distance is often a few metres in length. If you caused ripples in a pond with a large stick you could control the wavelength by how often you vibrated the stick.

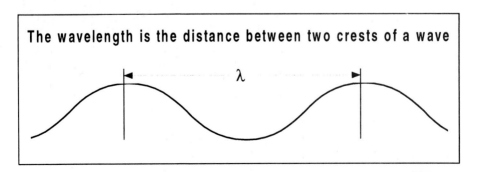

**The wavelength is the distance between two crests of a wave**

$\lambda$

How often something vibrates in one second is called the *frequency*. If you tap your desk once per second you would be tapping with a frequency of 1 Hertz (Hz). The sounds we hear are a result of vibrations in the air, causing the sound detectors in our ears to vibrate at the same frequency. The musical note 'middle C' is a sound with a frequency of 256 Hz, while if you go up an octave to high C the frequency doubles to 512 Hz. Sound is a form of wave motion that needs a medium like air, or water, to travel in. No medium no sound, it cannot travel in a vacuum.

There would be no point shouting on the moon. But if we had a radiolink to a moon dweller we could communicate with them. There are waves that can travel through the vacuum of space. Light from the sun is the most obvious form of this radiation but so also is the heat that comes from the sun and travels the 93 million mile distance just as quickly. How quickly? It can travel here in 8 minutes or 176,000 miles a second or, as scientists prefer in this metric age, 300 million metres per second ($3.10^8$ m/s) which is called the speed of light (c).

The radiations from the sun are separated into the visible waves that can be further split up into the spectacular colours of the rainbow, into infrared (IR) waves that,

while not visible to the eyes, are detected by us as heat, and the suntan and melanoma producing ultraviolet (UV) rays, also invisible, which continually stream through the supposedly ever thinning ozone layer. All of these are a subset of a family of radiations that can travel through space at the speed of light. This family is called the *electromagnetic* (EM) *spectrum*. They are given this name because they can have an effect on things that possess electrical or magnetic properties, such as atoms, and therefore living things which are made up of atoms.

Although IR, visible and UV are all of the same electric and magnetic nature and travel at the same speed they are obviously different in their properties and in the way we detect them. What makes them distinct to each other is that their wavelengths are different, which in turn means their frequencies are different.

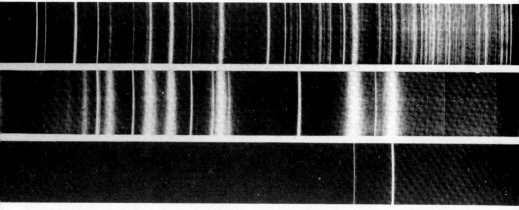

Just like waves on the sea, the longer the distances between them (wavelengths), the less often they pass by, meaning the smaller their frequency.

How do the three types of electromagnetic (EM) radiations coming from the sun differ? They have very short wavelengths and therefore high frequencies. Our eyes are only sensitive to a narrow range of EM wavelengths, from about 760 nanometres (nm) which we experience as red light down to about 400 nm which we experience as violet. If all the wavelengths between 760 and 400 nm fall onto the optical detectors in our eyes all the colours of the rainbow or prism will be mixed and we see white light. This happens with the wavelike rays from the sun or a tungsten halogen lamp hence they appear white. On the other hand almost all the waves coming from a neon advertising light come from the range around 700 nm and thus appears red.

The sun also pours out wavelengths that are higher and lower than this visible range. Wavelengths greater than red are called IR and those with smaller wavelengths than violet are called UV. These ranges are further subdivided into sections A, B and C, with A being closest to the visible region. UVA is just above the violet while UVC is the furthest away. This division of the UV range is important in understanding the health effects of UV radiation and they frequently feature on sun protection creams.

The EM family of radiation covers far more than these three important regions although it is only in the last hundred years that man has had any experience of the other members of the family. As one can see from the table on Page 56, overleaf, it would be hard to imagine living and enjoying modern life without access to the electromagnetic spectrum of radiations:

## The Electromagnetic Spectrum

gamma / X-ray   UV visible IR   microwaves   radiowaves   power lines

*short wavelengths/high frequency*   *long wavelengths/low frequency*

| REGION | SUBSECTION | WAVELENGTH | FREQUENCY | SOURCES |
|---|---|---|---|---|
| extremely low frequencies | ELF | 6000 km | 50 Hz | electric power lines and electric appliances |
| radio frequencies | very low-VLF | 100 km | 3 kHz | Loran-C mast |
| | medium-MF | 1000 m | 300 kHz | AM radio |
| *and* | very high-VHF | 10 m | 30 MHz | FM radio &TV mobile phones |
| microwaves | super high SHF extra high EHF | 1 cm 1 mm | 30 GHz 300 GHZ | microwave ovens radar |
| IR | IRC IRB IRA | 1 μm | 300 THz | lasers tungsten lamps the sun |
| Visible | RED YELLOW GREEN VIOLET | 750 nm 600 nm 500 nm 400 nm | $5.10^{14}$ Hz $6.10^{14}$ Hz | lasers, neon lamps the sun welding arcs fluorescent lamp |
| UV | UVA UVB UVC | 315 nm 280 nm 100 nm | $1.10^{15}$ Hz $3.10^{15}$ Hz | fluorescent lamps the sun mercury lamps |
| X-rays & ionising rays | | 10 nm | $3.10^{16}$ Hz | television X-rays gamma rays |

*Note: The product of wavelength and frequency always gives the same answer: $3.10^8$, the speed of light.*

## Two Types of Radiation

All radiation waves, even sound, carry energy and when they interact with matter such as living tissue they either pass right through - are transmitted, give up some or all of this energy (are partially or fully absorbed), or bounce back from the object by reflection. Visible light is mainly reflected, which is why we can actually see people, while X-rays are partially absorbed and partially transmitted.

The energy that the radiations carry depends entirely on their frequencies. The higher the frequency the greater the energy. We can think of the wave as being a bundle of energy called a *photon*. The higher the wave frequency the greater the energy that the photon carries. Radio waves have very low energy, while microwaves have much higher energy, with X-rays and gammas having the greatest. Because the radiations are electromagnetic in nature they can effect things that are influenced by electric and magnetic forces, such as the atoms in tissue. An obvious the effect would be to cause an increase in the temperature of tissue because energy is absorbed. However, the radiations with higher frequencies than UVA have such energetic photons that when they encounter an atom they can *ionise* it. Such radiation is called ionising radiation and includes X-rays and gamma rays. People who might be exposed to these in their work must be shielded from them by good absorbing materials such as lead, or if there is plenty of space, as in a nuclear power station, by concrete or water ponds.

All other types of EM radiation are non-ionising radiation (NIR). At the start of the twentieth century technology was only limited to the low frequency NIR of radio transmission and electricity. With newer technologies came higher electromagnetic frequencies. It soon became apparent that these frequencies - microwaves and higher radio frequencies - could cause significant heating in animal tissue. Around 30 MHz seems to be a dividing line between radiations that cause obvious heating and those which don't.

The dangers of *ionising radiation* are, by and large, well defined, so it is easy to understand why the creation of ions causes biological cell damage. For most of this century it has been assumed that NIR, lacking the energy to cause ionisation, had no bio-effects except to produce heating or electric shocks. NIR due to electricity power lines, VDUs, electric blankets, mobile phones, microwave cookers, antennae, etc, are now the subject of much interest and speculation and very contradictory research findings. There is a growing, if still largely unheeded, body of opinion which suggests that NIR may have serious while subtle effects on humans. We will now turn our attention to a brief look at the nature and affects of non-ionising radiation. NIR is given a shorter treatment due to space limitations and because a full understanding of its impact on human health lies in the future.

If you remove the ionising X and gamma rays from the EM spectrum then you are left with the non-ionising radiations (NIR). There are many regions of NIR that generate public interest, including among them:

- **UV:** Which is associated with sun tanning.
- **Radio Frequency (RF):** Including microwave radiation, which is linked to microwave cookers, mobile phones, MMDS television transmission, radar and military communications.
- **Extremely Low Frequency (ELF):** Which is linked with powerlines and to electric appliances in the home.

NIR can be considered to be those electromagnetic (EM) radiations with wavelengths longer than 100 nm. The photons of NIR carry bundles of energy that are too small to cause ions. Ions can upset the DNA in cells and thus be carcinogenic. NIR should therefore be much less dangerous to health than ionising radiation. It is clear, therefore, that whatever health effects are caused by NIR the biological mechanisms involved must be different to those associated with X-rays or radioactive radiation.

Radiation of short wavelengths, such as UV and visible, have limited penetration into the human body and so the effects are to the skin and the eyes. Penetration is greater with longer wavelengths and the energy of microwaves, for example, can be deposited deep into the body just as they are deposited into a chicken in a microwave cooker. Very long wavelengths such as radio waves can actually pass through you, as they do the walls of a building, depositing very little energy. The effects of NIR can be categorised as follows:

- **Photochemical:** These are effects where the photons cause some chemical effect in the body due to the photons giving up their energies to the body's molecules. For each chemical effect there is a 'threshold' wavelength of photon energy, below which the effect does not take place. These effects occur in the UV and violet-green end of the visible and include sunburn, tanning, snow blindness and on the positive side, vitamin D formation.

• **Thermal:** At longer wavelengths (lower frequency or energy) there is not enough energy to cause chemical changes in the body and the most obvious effects are mainly thermal (due to heating). Excessive heating can cause disruption of proteins and enzymes. IR and microwave radiations fall into this category

• **Electrical effects:** These could include shocks and burns. The electric and magnetic fields associated with RF and ELF radiations can interfere with the normal operation of muscle and other cells in the body. Involuntary contraction of muscles as experienced at night can be caused by such effects. So also are the shocks one gets from touching car doors in summer.

## Ultra Violet Radiation

**"Tanorexia"** *Cosmopolitan*

"In the quest for all-year-round golden skin, an alarming number of people are tanning themselves to a cancerous death ... Fifty percent of malignant melanomas begin as moles"

**"Man's death prompts call for users to be told of sunbed risks"** *The Irish Times*

"A suntan generally is an indication of damage to the skin. It is the cumulative affect of ultraviolet on the skin that ultimately causes cancer. The more you get the greater the risk."

**"Hole in ozone threatens UK"** *Independent on Sunday*

"The ozone layer over Britain has suffered the worst damage ever recorded ... The ozone layer absorbs much of the harmful ultraviolet B radiation in the sun's rays"

Short-wave UV has enough energy to chemically change oxygen $(O_2)$ in the upper atmosphere into ozone $(O_3)$ which forms a protective belt called the ozone layer. The production of the ozone requires these high energy UV photons and therefore they are absorbed, rather than being transmitted to the lower altitudes. There are a number of effects of UV exposure including skin cancer, burns, cataracts and premature skin ageing. There are two types of skin cancer caused:

malignant melanomas which are comparatively rare (but increasing) in the western world and non-melanoma skin cancers (NMSK) which are rarely fatal. The risks seem to be associated with the cumulative lifetime dose of solar radiation. NMSKs are most associated with people of European origins living in sunny parts of the world such as California and Australia. No increase among Black Americans is evident, but there is a definite association between social class and incidence due to recreational practices. Health education bodies have become very aware of the risks of UV exposure from the sun and sunbed treatment.

UV has three subdivisions: A, B and C, based on the wavelengths. UVC (100-280 nm) is completely blocked out by the ozone layer. UVB (280-315 nm) are the burning rays and seem to be the cause of non-malignant melanomas while UVA (315-400 nm) which are the most penetrating due to their longer wavelengths are associated with premature ageing. It is not yet clear which type of UV radiation is most associated with malignant melanomas. UVB has the beneficial effect of producing vitamin D, but in Ireland as little as 15 minutes daily is sufficient for this healthy purpose. Sunbeds give out UVA and UVB. Some of the newer UVA lamps cause less burning, but don't forget the penetrating, and thus ageing, power of these rays.

## Exposing Celtic skin

Over-exposure to UV leads to erythema or sunburn of the skin. The dose of UV that just causes noticeable reddening of the skin is called one minimal erythemal dose (one MED). It is now recognised that there are different skin types in terms of sensitivity to UV.

Therefore one MED for a dark skinned person would be greater than for a fair skinned person. Skin types can be divided into 6 groups. Type 1 holds little consolation for Irish sun worshippers, as it is sometimes labelled 'Celtic skin' and is defined as very bright skin with freckles, reddish hair, never tans always burns. The classification extends through 6 types to dark skin that never burns. For most people of European origin it goes as far as type 4 for olive skin with a low inclination to burn.

So, although, the UV dose depends very much on the season, the time of day and the cloud cover it also depends on your skin type and the type of activity you are engaged in. A simple equation can be used to calculate the length of time that will give you a dose of one MED. The equation is: **AxBxC.** A is the time to get one MED if lying horizontally (which depends on the time of day and year). B is the skin type factor (0.8 for Celtic skin and 2.0 for olive skin). C is a prolongation factor for the type of activity (1 for lying horizontally, 2 for sea swimming, 4 for tennis or golf and 6 for gardening). Therefore, for a Celtic skinned Irish person going for a mid-day walk (C = 3) on a cloudless day during a central European holiday in July, the time required to get a dose of one MED would be AxBxC = 25 minutes x 0.8 x 3 = 60 minutes. If using a sun screen factor one multiplies this time by the factor. A sun factor of 5 should allow you to walk five hours, assuming that sun factors can be believed. The closer you are to the equator the shorter the time required to get one MED.

## The ozone layer

UVB rays are most predominant from 10 am to 3 pm, hence the regular advice to be careful during this time interval. UVA penetrates equally throughout the day. A depletion of the ozone layer would result in an increase in UVB, but have no effect on the UVA, which already penetrates to the ground. For penetration of UVC the ozone depletion would have to be catastrophic. Despite the commonly held view to the contrary the widely publicised ozone depletion cannot be fully responsible for the melanoma upsurge, as the amount of UVB penetrating in Europe and the US has not, in fact, increased very much. Melanoma, like other cancers has a long latency period of 10-20 years, which means that ozone depletion hasn't been around long enough to play a significant role. Melanomas have been on the increase since the Second World War and the increase is probably more related to greater awareness of the disease and to recreational practices.

## *Power Line Radiation*

**"Growing doubts on power pylon 'link to cancer'"**

*Irish Independent*

"... research may help to explain the increased incidence of cancer associated with electromagnetic fields from electric wiring and overhead power cables"

Just as the world of 'conscious' radioactivity was 100 years old in 1996 the modern era of electrical technology could be dated from Edison's electric light bulb or perhaps the opening of his electricity generating station in New York in 1882. This was a low voltage *DC (direct current)* system which could only be transmitted short distances. By 1894 Nicola Tesla was supplying the city of Buffalo with an *AC (alternating current)* system, powered by Niagara Falls. AC systems are now the norm. In Europe the AC voltage and current varies (changes direction) 50 times a second giving it a frequency of 50 Hz. This is a frequency not found in the natural EM spectrum on earth.

In fact, prior to the age of electricity there were entire regions of the EM spectrum that did not exist. The natural EM *fields* consisted of visible light, IR and UV, along with occasional lightning strikes and low frequency fluctuations in the earth's magnetic field. Now, we have ourselves created an electromagnetic jungle, with EM radiation of almost every frequency in the EM spectrum. We are at swim in a sea of energy that is largely man-made. These artificial radiations have made modern living; radio, TV, mobile telephones, radar, fast cooking, etc, a reality. Is it possible that some of these unnatural energies are harmful?

## AC/DC electricity

It is certainly hard to imagine the modern world without the existence of electrical energy. In Europe domestic or mains electricity is supplied at an average voltage of about 220 to 240 *volts* (V). Unlike the constant steady voltage (DC) one gets from a battery the mains voltage (AC) changes, or alternates, direction 50 times a second (50 Hz). When a domestic appliance is plugged into a socket electrical current flows through the appliance (kettle, TV, etc) and delivers the energy. Electric currents are measured in *amps* and most are familiar with the rating of fuses in amps. A 13 amp fuse is used in the plug of an electric kettle or a microwave cooker because in normal operation the electric current flowing in the flex will be less than 13 amps and the fuse will not 'blow'. The greater the current the greater the energy delivered and thus the more powerful the appliance. *Power* is measured in *watts*. If one multiplies the voltage by current the answer equals the power of the device. A 220 W bulb would have approximately 1 amp (1 A) of current flowing through it. (220 V multiplied by 1 A gives 220W).

The energy is generated in electricity power stations and transmitted by transmission power lines from the generating stations via sub-stations to the consumers. To transmit the huge amount of electrical power that a typical modern town needs one must have either high voltages or high currents (power = voltage x current). If the transmission lines had high currents then a lot of energy would be lost to the atmosphere by the current heating the wires as it does an electric heater. For this reason transmission power lines operate at high voltages, up to 400 kV in Ireland. It is necessary to reduce these dangerous high voltages down to the low value we use in our homes, at a sub-station outside of towns. This is achieved by using transformers.

## Electric and magnetic fields

When electricity at any voltage flows through a wire the wire behaves as an aerial emitting electromagnetic (EM) radiation at a frequency of 50 Hz (60 Hz in the USA). This is often observed when one's car radio suffers interference driving under a power line. Household appliances also emit this EM radiation. Because the frequency is extremely low it is labelled ELF radiation and its wavelength measures 6,000 km. Because the wavelengths are so big nobody is ever far enough from an electrical current to say that the wire (antenna) is radiating or sending out its energy in a true wave-like manner. Therefore when investigating the effects of ELF 'radiation' one must measure the effects of the electric (E) and magnetic (M) aspects of the radiation separately. *(This is not necessary with higher frequency waves like microwaves or UV because their wavelengths are so small one is usually many wavelengths distant from the source or antenna. When that happens you are receiving true radiation and can ignore the separate E and M aspects. You can treat this radiation as consisting of wave-like packages or photons of energy)*

An 'electric field' is a region where a charged particle (like an electron) will be affected and made to move or vibrate. A 'magnetic field' is a region where a magnet will be made to move. Atoms and molecules which contain charges also behave like microscopic-magnets and will move or vibrate in electric and magnetic fields. Biological matter such as cells are made of atoms and molecules and therefore E and M fields could have biological effects.

Electric fields depend on the size of the voltage applied to a wire or a power line. They are measured in units of volts per metre (V/m). The magnetic fields depend on the amount of current flowing in a wire and are measured in units of amps per metre (A/m). A magnetic field only exists while current flows but the electric field still exists if an appliance, such as an electric blanket, remains plugged into the mains voltage. Magnetic fields are often measured in units named after the American engineer Tesla (T). American textbooks use another unit, called the Gauss (G). The relation between the various units is as follows:

**$1 \ \mu T = 0.8 \ A/m \ (= 1 \ mG)$**

As far as high voltage power lines are concerned the E and M fields are greatest directly underneath and diminish rapidly with distance from the lines. The highest voltage power cables in Ireland are the 400 kilovolt lines carrying energy from the Moneypoint generating station, in County Clare, to the capital city. Directly beneath a 400 kV line the ground level E fields could reach up to 11 kV/m while the M field can have maximum values of 30 A/m (40 μT). Lower voltage lines produce weaker fields. Electric blankets can produce E fields in the range 0.1 - 1 kV/m and M fields from 0.5 - 10 μT. Electric razors produce similar E fields but, due to their internal motors, produce M fields that are ten times higher than electric blankets. In terms of potential health hazards one must also take into account the length of time one is in close proximity to either device. A razor is only used for a few minutes daily but electric blankets can be on all night.

In our discussion of radioactivity we encountered the idea of a natural background level of radioactivity in our environment and we can use the average exposure as a reference to compare other exposures, be they artificial as in the case of Sellafield discharges, or natural, as in the case of radon. There are also natural E and M fields in our environment. There is a layer of charged particles and ions, known as the ionosphere, surrounding our earth. This creates an E field which in fine weather measures about 100 V/m. In thunder storms one gets huge electrical activity in the atmosphere and this natural E field can become many thousands of volts per metre. Also the earth behaves like a magnet which is why compasses point to the north or south. This creates an M field which in Ireland has a strength of about 35 amps per metre (A/m) or about 45 micro Tesla (μT).

Both of these natural fields are fairly steady (DC) and do not change direction. The north magnetic pole does not alternate and become the south magnetic pole, although this seems to have happened a few times since the beginning of the universe (but not recently). Radioactive rays of similar energy from a natural and an artificial source will be identical and capable of identical health consequences. On the other hand while the natural E and M fields can often have values much higher than man-made appliances there is one big difference.

The bulk of artificially produced fields are alternating or continually vibrating. Natural fields tend to be DC and artificial fields are usually AC. This difference may become very significant as our understanding of the subtle interplay between EM fields and the bio-electricity of the body becomes better understood.

Normally with health hazards and toxic materials 'more is worse'. More is certainly worse for polluting chemicals in water or in air pollution. It is usually worse with radioactivity. In the case of EM fields there are suggestions that sometimes less can be worse. There are studies that show that some cell functions, those that are not affected by strong fields, respond to lower field strengths. Similarly, the response may depend on the frequency - and not the strength - of a field. This latter effect is an example of resonance, where vibrations can be magnified when an applied frequency or rate of vibration matches the natural vibration of the object.

A familiar example of this resonant effect is the ease with which you can push a child up in the air when playing on a swing. It a question of timing, you must apply your push to match the vibration of the swing. Resonance effects might explain why biological effects occur in the body at low EM energies where they might not be expected.

Because the E and M fields can cause charges to move, the effect of them is to induce small electric currents to flow in electricity conducting materials like metals and people. If you hold a fluorescent bulb in your hands and stand under a high voltage power line the E field can be great enough to make the bulb glow. It may also be felt by your hair vibrating or cause the shock you sometimes get in summer when you touch your car. M fields also cause currents to flow in the body but these are usually imperceptible by the body.

An electric current of about 1 mA from hand to hand is on the threshold of perception. If one stood under a power line with an E field of 1 kV/m a current of about 15 $\mu$A is caused to pass through your feet. This current will be doubled if the field is doubled in size. Even if the current was 100 $\mu$A this would cause a current density (the amount of current flowing through a cross-section of the body) of about 2 mA per square metre (2 mA/m$^2$). Natural muscle activity in the body frequently creates current densities of about 10 mA/m$^2$. The current densities induced by M fields are a lot less than for E fields with a field of 10 $\mu$T giving rise to current densities of about 40 $\mu$A/m$^2$.

## Exposure limits

At this stage of our knowledge it is difficult to decide what aspect of the interaction of EM fields with the body should be taken as a measure of dose or exposure, because the interactions are complex and not well understood. Some well established effects - such as the electrical behaviour of nerve and muscle cells - show a dependence on current density. Thus, because thresholds for these effects can be demonstrated, current density is chosen by the International Radiation Protection Association (IRPA) as the basis for their limits on exposure to the E and M fields due to 50 Hz radiation. The aim is to limit current densities in the head and torso due to exposure to these E and M fields to no more than $10 \text{ mA/m}^2$ which is a typical naturally occurring value in the adult body. The IRPA have thus recommended the following exposure limits for 50 Hz exposure:

| Exposure | E Field | M Field |
|---|---|---|
| Occupational | 10 kV/m | 0.5 mT |
| General Public | 5 kV/m | 0.1 mT |

It is worth noting that the IRPA in setting these limits state that they are based on known effects and whereas they mention that epidemiological studies suggest an association between exposure to 50 Hz fields and cancer they note that the association is unproven. Therefore these studies are not taken to provide any basis for risk assessment useful for the development of exposure limits.

In 1990 the Environmental Protection Agency (EPA) in the US concluded in a draft report that ELF magnetic fields are 'probable human carcinogens' and classified them in the same risk category as DDT. After intervention by US government officials this was changed to 'possible' human carcinogens. This report was later abandoned and a new committee set up that concluded that there was insufficient evidence to prove an adverse health link.

In 1993 the Swedish National Electrical Safety Board in an interim report summarised that there is a strong suspicion of a link between ELF magnetic field exposure and childhood leukaemia, a reasonable suspicion of a link between occupational exposure and cancer in adults and a weak suspicion of a link between residential field exposure and cancer in adults. They stated that new schools, care centres and play groups should not be located in areas exposed to ambient magnetic fields above 0.2 µT, 500 times less than the above IRPA limit for the general public.

A simple method to get a qualitative measure of the existence and size of the EM fields close to electrical appliances is to use a simple battery operated AM radio. Tune the radio to a spot on the dial with no station and turn up the volume. As you approach an appliance the level of noise will increase. As you move away the noise will decrease and where it disappears the field strength will be roughly 0.1 µT.

*(Electric shocks depend on the current that flows in your body. Electric current flowing through vital organs such as the heart or brain can severely effect their operation. It can also heat tissue and cause burns. When it stimulates the nerves and the muscles we call it shock. Most people can experience an electric current of 1mA but a current of over 10 mA can cause severe muscular contraction that may prevent release of the source of electricity. Currents of 70 mA through the torso causes ventricular fibrillation of the heart muscles and death.)*

## *Microwave Radiation*

The region of the electromagnetic spectrum with frequencies from 300 kHz to 300 GHz is given the generic term of radiofrequency or RF. The subsection from 300 MHz to 300 GHz (wavelengths from 1 m to 1 mm) is more usually called the microwave region.

Microwaves find many uses, from telecommunications to industrial heating, to medical diathermy in physiotherapy, to the ubiquitous domestic cooker. The frequencies of some familiar technological applications are given in the following table:

| | |
|---|---|
| Proposed LORAN C marine navigation system | 100kHz |
| RTE Radio 1 | 88MHz |
| UHF Television | 700MHz |
| GSM mobile phones | 900 MHz |
| Microwave ovens | 2.45 GHz |
| MMDS TV distribution system | 2.66GHz |
| Police traffic radar | 10GHz |

Unlike very low frequency radiation, like ELF, which passes through the body microwave radiation is absorbed by the body. The most obvious and best documented biological effects of RF and microwave radiation on the body are thermal in origin. The health risk is considered to depend on the rate at which this thermal energy is absorbed by the body and how quickly the body can regulate or dispose of this extra energy. The rate of energy absorption is called the '*specific absorption rate*' (*SAR*) and is measured in units of *watts* (or milliwatts, mW) per unit mass or per kilogram. In other words, how much energy per second (joules per second or watts) is absorbed by a kilogram of body tissue. Where the body cannot dispose of this thermal energy burns and damage could ensue. The eye is a region that is unable to eliminate heat quickly and hence the possibility of cataract formation.

The SAR concept is a useful and simple way of quantifying the interactions of RF radiation with living organisms.

A person doing physical exercise can generate 3-5 *W/kg* (watts per kilogram) and probably perspires profusely to eliminate this thermal energy. Even at rest our bodies produce heat at a rate up to 100 W (like a 100 W bulb) which would be equivalent to 2 W/kg in a 50 kg person. An SAR of 1-4 W/kg for thirty minutes would produce a temperature rise of less than 1 degree Celsius in a healthy adult. Such a rise in temperature should pose no problems for the human thermoregulatory system of healthy adults.

The guideline for RF exposure is based on this knowledge and set lower as a safety factor. The restrictions on exposure recommended by the IRPA are as follows. The average SAR, in the body over any six minute period, for those occupationally exposed to RF is set at 0.4 W/kg and is 20 times less for the general public at 0.08 W/kg. Allied with this is that the maximum value of SAR for any 0.1 kg (the weight of a tin of sardines) of tissue, excluding hands and feet, should not exceed 10 W/kg.

Up to the 1980s thermal effects resulting from RF and microwave exposure were the only effects considered. Possible non-thermal biological effects were largely ignored. There were many incidences of complaints of vague ailments from people who work close to radio and radar transmitters. These were always put down to radiation induced heating. Safety standards had still to be developed for these effects. It was calculated that a dose of a tenth of a watt or 100 mW of power to an area of one square centimetre, of skin (less than the area of a small stamp) would be greater than the ability of the blood's circulation system to remove the heat. This can be written as $100 \text{ mW/cm}^2$.

Applying a safety factor of 10 led to a dose limit of $10 \text{ mW/cm}^2$ (or $100 \text{ W/m}^2$) established in the USA in 1966. It is worth noting that this level of exposure is equivalent to a whole body exposure of about 100 W as the surface area of an adult body is about one square metre ($1 \text{m}^2$). Such a heat exposure would not be expected to increase the body's temperature noticeably. An electric bar heater gives out 2,000 W. At some microwave frequencies the limits are now lower than this 1966 figure.

Waves in the FM radio band (around 100 MHz) have wavelengths of about the same dimensions as humans and this could lead to greater absorption by people of these waves. As a result the dose limits for these radiations were therefore reduced in the 1980s. However the standards were still based on the thermal effects alone.

## Microwave ovens

For frequencies greater than 30 - 100 MHz the dominant interaction with tissue is the deposition of heat. Food and human tissue is largely composed of molecules of water, $H_2O$, which are electrical in nature. Put simply, the electric and magnetic nature of the electromagnetic microwave radiation causes these molecules to vibrate at the frequency of the radiation. It is the friction caused by these vibrations that gives the heating effect. (Just as the friction of rubbing your hands on a cold day has a heating effect). Interestingly, you can't melt a dry ice cube in a microwave oven, because the $H_2O$ molecules in ice are all linked together, and are therefore unable to vibrate.

Microwave cooking is used because of the speed with which food can be heated. In conventional cooking, using gas or electricity, the oven, its walls and the air inside have to be heated. This heat energy is then transferred from the hot air to the food surface and then by conduction into the interior. This process is both energy inefficient and slow. Cooking with microwaves all the energy is absorbed by the food and the oven interior is not heated at all, a fact that can be verified by feeling the oven walls after you have taken out the cooked food. Furthermore, microwaves penetrate 1-3 cm below the surface of the food - hence the notion that they cook from the inside out.

The main danger associated with domestic ovens is the possibility of microwaves leaking out through the door of the oven. For this reason all microwave cookers ensure that the generation of microwaves is stopped whenever the door is opened. The main precaution for the user is not to damage the door and to keep the oven clean, so as to minimise the risk of leakage.

While microwave leakage in a properly maintained microwave cooker is negligible, it is not zero. Some international standards for maximum leakage at a distance of 5 cm from new ovens are set at 5 mW/cm$^2$ - while the US Food and Drug Administration (FDA) value is 1 mW/cm$^2$. The FDA suggest that higher levels of microwaves could be dangerous. This value of *power density* drops rapidly with distance being less than a third of this value at 30 cm and 500 times less at a metre. Keeping your distance from any source of radiation is one of the best means of reducing your exposure. Many surveys have found that up to half the microwave cookers over two years in use leaked radiation greater than 5 mW/cm$^2$.

## Transmitters and receivers

> ### "Garda agrees to allow new mobile phone service use its masts" *The Irish Times*
>
> "In July, Esat Digiphone said it had planning permission for only 70% of the masts it was trying to erect...The use of Garda masts will speed up its efforts to reach its target"
>
> ### (Minister)"wants masts to be located away from residential areas" *The Irish Times*
>
> "Telecommunications masts should be sited near residential areas only as a last resortunder new guidelines for planning authorities published by the Department of the environment"

**The intensity of a beam decreases as one moves away from the source**

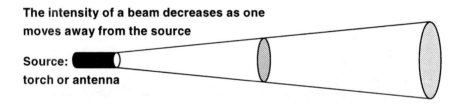

**Source:** torch or antenna

If you shine a torch in the dark the light gets less bright or intense as you move away from the torch. This is because the energy radiating from the torch is spreading out over a larger area. We can therefore measure *intensity* in terms of the amount of energy per second (Watts) that passes through a given area, such as a square metre ($m^2$) or a square centimetre ($cm^2$). Thus, intensity is measured in $W/m^2$ or often in $mW/cm^2$. 1 $W/m^2$ equals 0.1 $mW/cm^2$. It is the same measure for masts transmitting RF and microwave radiation, whether for mobile phones, TV, radar, marine navigation, army communications, local radio, etc. This quantity is called the *power density*.

There are many different bodies that set exposure guidelines and these can vary somewhat from country to country. The IRPA power density guidelines for public exposure are 0.2 $mW/cm^2$ for the lower radio frequencies that have wavelengths similar in dimension to human size (eg, VHF or FM frequencies) and 1 $mW/cm^2$ for the higher frequency microwaves.

It can be hard to visualise these strange units. If you lay out in the summer sun at noon you would receive in the order of 500 W (over 100 mW/cm²) on your body although only a fraction of this would be RF, as sunlight consists mainly of IR and visible radiation with some UV.

It is worth noting that Ireland has no regulations or agency dealing with exposure limits for NIR. Most experts use the IRPA guidelines when discussing exposure from microwaves. The NRPB in the UK have set their limits ten times higher for the microwave region of the electromagnetic spectrum while the former Soviet Union had a much lower set. SAR values are difficult to measure and so power density values (easily monitored) derived from them are frequently used when discussing exposure from microwaves. The SAR of 0.08 W/kg, set for the general public, is taken as being equivalent to an exposure from microwaves of about 0.5 mW/cm². These limits are set to provide adequate protection from thermal effects, even if radiation from a number of microwave sources are combined.

## MMDS

**"TV mast proximity 'not a cancer risk'** *Irish Independent*

"The incidence of leukaemia near 20 high power transmitters was studied by ... a scientific group set up to investigate clusters of disease which might be linked with environmental pollution. The unit reported no excess risk of leukaemia within 2 km of the transmitter masts ... but did find an excess of leukaemia at one site ..."

Multipoint Microwave Distribution System (MMDS) transmitters have been the subject of concern and opposition in various parts of the country although sometimes it appears that protest is orchestrated by operators and users of TV deflector systems. The Tonabrucky mast, near Galway city, is a typical example of an MMDS system and it transmits with a microwave frequency of 2.6 GHz. At this frequency the IRPA exposure guideline is 1 mW/cm².

As you increase your distance from a transmitter the power density of the radiation decreases. At a distance of 100 m from the mast the power density is a million times less than the IRPA guideline at 1 nanometre /cm² while at Rahoon, a distance of three kilometres away, it has dropped to over 200 billionths of this limit.

The power of the MMDS transmitter near Coolaney in County Sligo is described as being 20 W per television channel. It is important to realise that the effect of various radiations that one is exposed to is cumulative. Unlike a TV set that can be tuned to one channel at a time an exposed person receives the energy from all the channels. So if this transmitter is transmitting 15 TV channels then its power is 300 W. As in the Galway case exposure drops rapidly with distance and thermal effects should not pose a problem.

Interestingly Ireland is the only European country with a nationally based MMDS system because around Europe this 2.5 GHz band of frequencies is used for military communication. The Irish were able to use the 2.6 GHz American system, which was readily available as the Irish army uses lower frequency wavebands such as VHF and HF. Some continental countries are experimenting with MMDS frequencies of around 40 GHz.

## Mobile phones

### "Antennae report alarms school" *Sligo Champion*

" We would have the most serious objections to the siting of this base station at Sligo garda station if it involves the risk of health hazard from continuous microwave exposure ... the siting of masts/base stations near centres of population, institutions and above all schools give cause for grave concern and alarm"

### "Cell phone threat to pacemakers" *Sunday Tribune*

"The general advice is that if you have a pacemaker never carry your phone in your breast pocket ... Mobile phones pump out strong radiowaves which can penetrate the body cavity, and any metal object inside will pick up the waves. The radio signal pulses 250 times a second, while the pacemaker beats once a second. If it is told to beat 250 times a second, the heart could theoretically become confused"

Mobile phones operate in the RF-microwave region. The Eircell and Esat GSM mobiles use a frequency of about 900 MHz. They operate as two-way radios. A transmitter or antenna sends out a signal and the mobile phone that receives the signal in turn transmits back to the antenna. These systems operate in *'line of sight'*, hence the need for the many cellular phone antennae which now dot the countryside at intervals of about 15 miles in the case of Telecom's Eircell system. As the antennae radiate energy they do so at so many joules of energy per second (or watts). The Esat system transmits with a power of approximately 300 W or less and they are to be built at a height of 37 m in rural areas and 20 m in urban areas. Note that they are less powerful than the average microwave cooker which is usually rated in the 600 W to 1000 W range. This is a low power transmitter when you realise that RTE's UHF-TV transmitter at Cairnhill, County Longford has a power of 800 kW (at a frequency 700 MHz) and a local radio station, like *104 FM* in Dublin, transmits with a power of 10 kW (at 104 MHz).

The further you are from the antenna or transmitter the less the power density of the radiation and hence the less your exposure. Fifty metres from a 300 Watt Esat transmitter the power density will have dropped to about 1/500 of the IRPA guideline while at 500 m it will be ten times less again. A properly designed and built cellular antenna, 20 m high and operating at full power, might produce a power density of $0.02 \text{ mW/cm}^2$ on the ground near the antenna site, but usually this will be a lot less. These guidelines could be violated if people gained entry to the site and mounted the antenna or if the antenna were mounted on or near roofs of existing buildings in built up areas.

Esat Digifone have had some difficulty in obtaining planning permission for some of its masts. This problem will be partly solved by using already existing Garda masts. There is a growing trend to cluster various antennae for different purposes. Although the frequencies in these clusters vary, depending on the application, the energies emitted are cumulative in any exposed person. Many of these clusters

are in built up areas and will have people living and working quite close to the boundaries of the antennae sites.

The power of a mobile phone handset ranges between 2 W and 8 W, depending on the type or class of the mobile. The Esat and Eircell digital handsets have a power of 2 W. Their receivers, which are held close to the head, could deposit up to 50% of their microwave energy into the head. Will these microwaves 'cook your brain' or cause '*hot spots*' inside your head?

Although the power density of radiation propagating through the air is easily measured it is important to know how this microwave radiation interacts with the inside of the head. Because the structure of the head is anything but homogenuous it is possible that microwave energy will not be uniformly absorbed and perhaps there will be hot spots. Doses to the head are estimated by using a model of the human head, called the 'phantom' head, which is a fibreglass shell filled with an appropriate liquid to simulate the head. SAR values for different parts of the head can be measured. The SAR values obtained can be then compared with the exposure guidelines of bodies such as the IRPA.

Interestingly, the more recently established International Commission on Non-Ionising Radiation Protection (ICNIRP) in recognising the possibility of localised absorption of radiation, 'hot spots', recommends that, for workers, the previous 10 W/kg limit averaged over 100 gram of tissue, should now be averaged over 10 g. Furthermore they recommend that while the whole body limit remains at 0.08 W/kg for the general public, the limit averaged over a 10 g mass should be 2 W/kg.

Doses of SAR obtained can depend on many factors including the power of the handset, the type of aerial, distance from head, mode of operation, etc. Research findings seem to vary a lot, with some results significantly exceeding the guidelines, particularly those for the general public. What is definitely obvious from a review of research literature is that most estimated SAR doses to the head are not significantly lower than the IRPA limits for thermal effects. This may not necessarily be a problem as the IRPA limits are set at 'thermal' dose levels that the normally functioning adult body can supposedly deal with.

When two people are having a conversation they usually talk at equal loudness. It is the same for the GSM base station and the individual mobile. Thus for the efficient working of GSM networks the strength of the signal from the mobile to the base station attenna should equal that received by the mobile from the base station. This will be of the order of 3 W for a single user (channel). It is obvious from this that a mobile phone beside a user's head generates a far greater exposure than that emanating from standing at the bottom of, say, a 15 m high Eircell tower.

Average power densities from typical mobile units have been quoted by the Department of Transport, Energy and Communications at 0.45 mW/cm$^2$ which is very close to the IRPA exposure limits for the general public. Remember that averages mean that many of the exposure values will be greater than this figure. The author has recorded microwave intensities at mobile aerials that exceed what would be considered unacceptable leakage from a microwave oven. It appears that far greater concern should be directed at exposure from the handsets rather than that from the cellular towers. The aerial on the mobile should be kept as far away from the head as possible. Perhaps, along with the cost this is an added incentive to keep calls short.

## Army Surveillance

> ## "RUC radio 'link in cancer deaths' " *The Sunday Times*
>
> "Three members of a secret RUC surveillance unit have died suddenly from cancer, prompting allegations that their deaths may be linked to concealed radio transmitters worn by undercover detectives ... all had worn concealed radio or microwave transmitters as part of their work"

One of the most controversial issues involving NIR radiation in this country is the array of communication and surveillance equipment operated by the British army in the South Armagh area. The presence of such a range of electronic equipment has led to a lot of local disquiet and the suggestion of local cancer clusters and other inexplicable events such as discolouring of hedgerows. Requests to the army and the UK parliament for detailed information on this equipment have fallen on deaf ears under the guise of secrecy. A request by the author to the British army HQ in Lisburn for information on power levels was answered with a 'news release' that claimed that all emissions were far below internationally recognised safety thresholds and were also less powerful that many domestic appliances.

Radiation sources fall into three categories in the press release. (i) IR radiation at powers of 300-500 W which is less than the ordinary domestic 2 kW electric bar heaters. (ii) Radio waves at powers similar to those used by citizen band radio (CB) enthusiasts. (iii) Radar which is claimed to be far less powerful than that used in air traffic control. It is pointed out that the security forces would be exposed to greater emissions than the residents due to their closer proximity to the equipment.

Signals equipment used by the Irish army has been inspected in conjunction with the Health and Safety Authority and all has been found to be well below recommended international limits. Use of radar by the Irish army is limited to their aerodrome and to the artillery corp. The army safety regulations advise that the danger area with the radar scanners are within a metre of the scanner. X-rays can be produced by high powered radar (45 kW) but again the suggested danger area is close to the equipment. This data may lend some credence to the British army claims in their news release but they posses a broader spectrum of equipment some of which is specifically dedicated to surveillance.

As with all radiation emitters the exposure from these sources should drop below the international guidelines if one maintains a reasonable distance from the antennae. This, of course, assumes that radiation is spreading out over a wider area with increasing separation from the transmitter. If very narrow beams are being used then the power will not decrease as rapidly with distance although less people will be exposed to the beam. Power densities from radar can be very high.

A survey of radar emitters in the US in the 1970s found over 20,000 capable of producing a power density of $10 \, mW/cm^2$ at a distance of 10 m and nearly another 600 that could produce this level at a 1 km distance. Normally the general public are not exposed to this type of radiation as it is usually emitted in an elevated trajectory. Population exposure from common RF/radar sources such as airport, marine and police radar is well below the IRPA limits. Police radar transmits a power of about 0.1 W giving power densities of less than $1 \, \mu W/cm^2$ at a distance of 30 m.

The secrecy shown by the army is regrettable, especially if the exposure levels are below international guidelines. In the absence of information rumours will abound and a variety of explanations for the unexplained will fill the vacuum, especially in a situation where a great deal of mistrust already exists. If cancer clusters exist in South Armagh they may be due to NIR, but they equally well may have a number of other factors, stress being an obvious candidate. Even given all the available information it would be difficult to decide the cause. Stating what the power and frequency bands of the radiation are would seem unlikely to jeopardise security.

## Loran C

> ### "Wales considered as alternative site for navigation mast"
> #### *The Irish Times*
>
> "Supreme court ruling rejected Loop Head site. The ruling not only affects the mast project (the Loran C mast was to be 720 feet high) - which aroused considerable opposition in Co. Clare - but delays development of this navigational network throughout northern Europe"

Another transmitter that received much (successful) opposition is the LORAN C Trans-European system for marine navigation which was planned for Loop Head in south west Clare. The frequency of operation is 100 kHz which is in the very low frequency region (which is below the 30-100 MHz division where one becomes concerned with thermal effects). Here the wavelengths are of the order of 3 km, which is twice the wavelength of BBC *Radio 4*, on the long wave band.

The people who would be most exposed to VLF would live within a wavelength (3 km) of the mast and are thus not receiving waves (or photons) of radiation. Instead, as with power line radiation (ELF), one must refer to and measure the electric and magnetic fields separately (rather than power densities). The LORAN C site would have had a site boundary at 300 m from the mast. Here the electric field would have been 40 V/m dropping to 10 V/m at the nearest house, 800 m away and to 5 V/m at a distance of 1 km. 40 m from the mast the E field would measure 250 V/m. The American ANSI exposure guidelines for this frequency are 614 V/m for occupational and public exposure. The IRPA guidelines for the public are far more stringent at 205 V/m. The exposure outside the site boundary would have been well below these exposure limits.

## Visual Display Units (VDUs)

Radiation from video display units has been associated with many ailments and effects among which rate of miscarriage features prominently. The variety of radiations from visual display units are similar to those from TVs. The main difference is that one is usually seated further away from TVs than from VDUs and distance is a critical factor in exposure reduction. VDUs emit ionising X-rays from the screen but these are 'soft' X-rays and do not penetrate the leaded glass in the screen. Visible light is obviously emitted as is IR in the form of heat.

Because a TV picture is made up of dots of light caused by an 'electron gun' in the TV tube it is necessary to move the dots, and hence the electron gun, very quickly across and down the screen to make the picture look continuous. These horizontal and vertical sweeps of the electron gun need to happen at speeds of less than milliseconds and hence sweep frequencies of 15-35 kHz are used leading to EM emmissions at these frequencies. As the frequency of the mains is 50 Hz ELF radiation at this frequency is also produced. Operators at a distance of 50 cm are typically typically exposed to an E field of less than 10 V/m and magnetic field values less than 0.1 μT. The Swedish government have recommended a limit of 0.25 μT measured half a metre in front of the VDU.

Statements by international bodies such as the IRPA (1988), WHO (1987) and ILO (1991) have stated that on the basis of current biomedical knowledge that there are no health hazards associated with VDUs. Yet work in Scandinavia suggests that women who work with VDUs giving off high levels of VLF and ELF and who spend long hours at VDUs have a greater miscarriage incidence. A relation between VDUs and brain tumours has also been reported. There are numerous such studies in all these EM radiation regions. Who does one believe?

According to the WHO the average value for RF background exposure in the US to the public is of the order of 5 nanowatts per centimetre squared ($5\ nW/cm^2$) with less than 1% of the population exposed to ambient power densities greater than 1 microwatt/cm² ($1\ \mu W/cm^2$). These values are one thousandth and almost one millionth of the IRPA exposure limits. VHF and UHF are the main contributors to these background exposures. The situation in Ireland would not be any worse than in the US, although with the recent increase in FM stations and cellular phone antennae the background levels will inevitably increase.

Although most of the radiation emitted by our bodies is through heat, in the IR region, a small amount is in the microwave/RF region of the EM spectrum. This amount of RF radiation is about 100 times greater than the environmental background of artificial RF. This type of comment is frequently used in order to calm people's worries about radiation, but it is important to realise that it is not the average background values one should worry about, but the higher power densities found close to sources of radiation.

# *Research into NIR*

Still people worry. Maintaining a 'reasonable' distance from transmitters will keep your exposure well below the international limits but these are only based on the possible thermal/heating effects. Other athermal biological effects are largely ignored in spite of the growing number of studies to testify to their possible reality. One hears stories of army men who didn't wish to have any more babies standing in front of their transmitters. The testes are so sensitive to temperature that such a comment may not be apocryphal. EM radiation has been associated with a wide range of biological risks including sterility, miscarriage, birth defects, cot deaths, hormonal changes, effects on immune system, fatigue and many others. Add to these possible association with cancer and leukaemia and some of the more recent diseases like AIDS, ME and autism and it is easy to understand why there is a lot of public disquiet.

The widely held view of those bodies who recommend exposure guidelines is that most of the established effects of RF fields are consistent with heating, resulting in rises in tissue or body temperatures greater than one degree Celsius. Studies that have highlighted athermal biological risks fall into three categories

**1) in vitro:** This type of research is laboratory based and involves exposure of individual cells or organs to EM radiation. Many effects have been found. Among them is the 'melatonin hypothesis'. Melatonin is secreted by the pineal gland and is critical to the circadian rhythms that govern daily functions of the body, such as alertness and sleep. It is suggested that ELF can adversely affect the production of melatonin and thus our health. In vitro research has shown that ELF fields can affect the flow of biologically important mineral ions, such as calcium and sodium, across cell membranes. Some of this research suggests that such cellular effects can occur within certain frequency windows (1-100 Hz) and sometimes within certain power density windows. Such data challenges the usual notion that the severity of an effect increases with size of dose.

Such findings are surprising as the accepted wisdom has been that the energy of ELF is far too low to effect the the separation of atoms or ions. In the 1980s a theory was put forward that might hold an answer. It claims that the ELF fields act in concert with the earth's geomagnetic field to produce a magnified resonant effect called cyclotron resonance. This concentration of energy could be sufficient to initiate major biological effects. In vitro research is important in the search for an explanatory mechanism to link EM radiation and fields to health effects. Until such mechanisms, as cyclotron resonance, are found and scientifically confirmed the issue of the athermal biological effects of EM radiation and fields will find great difficulty in gaining mainstream scientific legitimacy. It is, however, difficult to extrapolate from in vitro work to the behaviour of complex organisms such as animals and man. Hence the need to examine this area using *in vivo* research.

**2) in vivo:** Experiments with animals are very expensive and time consuming as one may need generations of animals to observe trends. Frequently these experiments have been badly designed, often do not lead to conclusions that are statistically significant and have proved hard to replicate.

The WHO in a recent summary of in vivo research state that most of the biological effects due to RF exposure reported are consistent with the responses due to induced heating resulting from tissue or body temperatures greater that 1°C and for SAR values above 1-2 W/kg. Above these temperatures, for example, animal studies show adverse effects in the implantation and growth of embryos and fetuses and in male fertility. They state that the overwhelming evidence is that RF exposure is not mutagenic, cancer initiating, but there is a possibility that high SAR exposures might act as tumour promoters.

**3) epidemiological:** These are studies on human populations that seek an association between exposure and various illnesses or disease. Occupational groups have been the principal sources of these data, eg, VDU operators, radar workers and so on. Association does not imply cause. There is a correlation between cocks crowing in the morning and the daily rise in temperature but it is not a causal relationship. Yet it is a number of epidemiological studies that have galvanised most of the concern in this area particularly concern on the connection between ELF power lines and cancer and childhood luekaemia.

Widely publicised studies are those of Wertheimer and Leeper in Denver and the more thorough study by Savitz where they report an increase in childhood leukaemia among children in homes close to heavy duty electricity distribution lines. Such studies are statistical in nature and as such have various uncertainties associated with them. The results can also be affected by the existence of confounding factors as it is impossible to find perfect control (exposure free) groups for comparative purposes. Also the incidence of childhood cancers and leukaemias in the general population is low (less than 1 in 1,000) so finding one or two excess cases in a study will have a major influence on the data although the result may be due to coincidence.

A major Swedish study involving over 100,000 children living close to high voltage power lines expecting to find 138 childhod cancers based on national rates found 142 cases, an excess of 4 among the studied group. These are typical of the figures found in this type of study. The relative risks found for exposure to higher fields are usually less than a factor of two. In comparison smoking has a lung cancer risk factor ranging from 20 to 60 times that of the non-smoker. Interestingly the WHO notes that, in studies of electrical workers, cancer effects seem more likely to be related to 50-60 Hz exposure, rather than to RF/microwave exposure.

VDU operators have received a lot of research interest, particularly the study of women of child bearing age. As already mentioned results are contradictory. Confounding problems such as job stress and ergonomics probably exist. The natural failure rate of pregancy is about 15% and, as always with random occurrences, clusters of such events can be expected. Again it is hard to find apparent relationships between size of dose or exposure to effect or response as one might expect with toxic agents.

Research results for EM radiation and fields do not lend themselves easily to simple conclusions about the resultant risks of exposure. The evidence is frequently conflicting and difficult to replicate. The evidence does not meet the stringent requirements of the scientific community, which seeks replication of findings, explanatory mechanisms, strong correlations, dose-response relations, experimental proof, etc. The scientific community has, however, been wrong in the past and indeed it is now accepted that scientific knowledge advances by the falsification of previous theories.

Science is not about hard edged certainties and there are some issues where its answers are based on the balance of probalility. The threat of EM radiation may be seen as a minor one yet it is one that nobody can totally refute. And so there are the seeds of doubt. The general public, often on the instigation of the media, have been bombarded with scare stories that when alligned to the general distrust of government pronouncement, business indifference to worker welfare and the lack of scientific understanding are left in a state of bewilderment.

Proponents of the hazardous nature of NIR paint the sceptical response of governments and the 'in denial' response of industry as being one of cover up and conspiracy. This is not surprising as we live in an age where big government and commerce seem to be in cohoots and frequently are found to be parsimonious with the truth. Yet despite the huge and increasing number of studies that are suggesting athermal biological effects from NIR it is a complex area abounding in confusion and often conflicting results. There are many factors involved:

- The difficulty of dealing with apparently inconsistent data and experimental results that are frequently hard to duplicate;
- The methodologies of many of the EMF studies may be flawed;
- The lack of convincing explanations for experimental results, the scientific establishment likes to have a theory or a mechanism for explanation;
- The relevance of results from animal experiments in controlled and often over-exposed conditions to the general public;
- The 'appeal to authority' in that so many august bodies are publicly unconvinced by the present evidence;
- The difficulty of measuring exposures accurately and the impossibility of finding control groups not exposed to EM radiation;
- Epidemiological studies can only point to associations and not causal links - there are so many confounding factors that can initiate or promote diseases such as cancer.

The public perception of risk is usually not based on statistics but on whether these risks are observable and controllable or vice versa. If they fall into the category of the mysterious and the invisible they tend to be overestimated. Hence EM radiation and fields are a good candidate for fear by the public and fear generation by the press.

With the present state of research and knowledge on the health issues associated with NIR and with the firm insistence of authorities that there is no consistent and conclusive evidence for athermal biological effects such as cancers and leukaemias, what, then, should be done? Further research is usually the answer. After this    we are into the realm of value judgements and this affords three options:

+ **Do Nothing:** If there is not sufficient evidence to suggest a real risk and to warrant any action.

+ **Prudent Avoidance:** If there is a basis for concern, which means efforts should be made to limit avoidable exposures, without excessive expenditure.

+ **Immediate limitation:** Spend large sums to limit exposure, although in the future the action may be proved unwarranted.

In the absence of any firm scientifically demonstrated connection between NIR and cancer the concept of 'prudent avoidance' has been invoked by many utility companies in the States especially in relation to ELF power lines. It has been defined as the exercise of sound judgement in practical matters. In the context of power lines it means keeping people away from exposure to strong fields when it can be done at a moderate cost but not to incur huge expense when the benefits are not obvious.

The costs of mitigating exposure to power line radiation are huge. Right of ways for transmission lines would have to be created at huge expense and the cost of redesigning cables and putting them underground would run into billions of pounds.

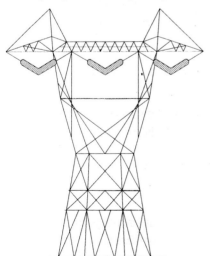

Already in the USA huge sums have been spent on efforts at mitigation and on divisive and lengthy legal proceedings.

Many prominent scientists are disturbed at this expenditure when the evidence for biological effects appears so scant. In 1988 the Russian scientist Andrei Sakharov, (the H-bomb is his legacy), evading questions on the bomb, cited the ecological threat to the environment as our most serious long term problem. He lamented the waste of large sums of public and private money on what he saw as a false threat (that of NIR on health).

In 1995 the Council of the American Physical Science Society stated that the scientific literature shows no consistent, significant link between cancer and power line fields. "More serious environmental problems are being neglected for the lack of funding and public attention, and the burden of the cost placed on the American public is incommensurate with the risk, if any."

If we want electricity we must have pylons and cables. If we want mobile phones we must have microwaves. If we want sun tanned bodies we must have UV sources. Would you forego the benefits for the risks?

## A question of proportion and information

### "High levels of carcinogens in Irish ham" *Sunday Tribune*

"Irish cooked ham contains a higher level of a potentially cancer-causing preservative than ham sold in other European countries, a new survey reveals"

### "Flying on a wing and a prayer" *Sunday Tribune*

"Jets crashed once every 9.8 days on average last year, and its going to get worse. Boeing, the world's biggest aircraft maker, predicts one major crash a week by 2010"

In relation to the risks posed by increased chronic exposure to low doses of ionising radiation there may be some uncertainities but with non-ionising radiation the jury is definitely still out. While some of the evidence on athermal effects is unconvincing, at present, this may change in the future when our knowledge of perhaps subtle interplays between radiation and biological systems improves beyond its present primitive levels. Present guidelines recommended by the various international bodies still provide a useful bench mark by which we can make some judgements as to what are acceptable and definitely unacceptable levels of exposure. Modern technology has definitely increased our burden of radiation but it is important to realise that we have always faced certain natural levels existing in the environment and often arising from within our own bodies.

We do not live in a risk free society. The increased risks have also to be placed in the context of the various benefits that come with technology. The risks of using medical ionising radiation are quantifiable, but the benefits are clear.

86

With our present level of knowledge it would be almost impossible, to similarly, quantify the risks of exposure to electromagnetic radiation and fields. In 1994 the Doll report in the UK concluded that if there are risks due to power line EM fields they would on present evidence be considered one of life's very small risks. A similar conclusion for microwaves could be expected from most 'expert' bodies. More people die from fireworks annually in the US than have died in 45 years of nuclear power operation in the US. Would you worry more about the dangers of BSE in beef or those of cooking it in your microwave? People will protest about the installation of a transmitter or power line, but do nothing to reduce their own exposure to domestic appliances or radon.

There is more public concern about mobile phone antennae, rather than the mobile phone handsets which yield greater exposure. More seriously, we have been lulled into a collective amnesia about the greatest risk of all, the anti-life exploitation by governments of all kinds of radiation for military purposes. Yes, we should be concerned about risks but we should not lose our sense of proportion.

## "CND claims people still at risk from 1958 incident"
*The Irish Times*

" ...there was a serious nuclear accident at the former US air base in 1958. the allegations centre around an incident at Greenham when a B47 caught fire. Live warheads containing uranium and plutonium exploded and contaminated dust scattered over the surrounding countryside".

## "The night nuclear bombs blazed in Berkshire" *The Observer*

"In 1957 a US bomber loaded with nuclear weapons exploded in the heart of England, poisoning a wide area. The Americans said it never happened. Then the British government conspired in the cover up. They are still lying ... The incidents include ... a second serious fire at Greenham Common in February 1958 ... A study ... was reopened into the unexplained leukaemia cluster among children living near the base".

Given the complexity of modern technology and the specialised nature of knowledge it is important for people to be informed. People have a right to know about any emmissions and developments that may affect their quality of life. As Clinton, the recently re-elected president of the US, has said:

" ... since the Community Right to Know Act has been on the books, reported reductions in toxic emissions are about 43% for the whole country. Now that's a law worth passing. No new bureaucracy; just power to the people through basic knowledge. This has kept millions of pounds of chemicals out of our lives. It has helped people to stay healthy and live longer ..."

If you are exposed to the risk then you should have the right to know. If you are going to proclaim a public position at least be informed. If you are going to take action join an environmental group such as Greenpeace, Friends of the Earth, the Green Party, CND etc. or set up your own local action group. Whereas these groups often seem to ignore mainstream scientific views they play a crucial role in pressurising governments and business to confront their responsibilities to the people and their environment. You can purchase monitors for measuring microwave power density and magnetic fields for less than £200 from a scientific instruments supplier. The RPII will carry out a radon test on your house for £15. Challenges based on emotions may be moving, ones based on numbers are harder to dismiss.

# C Understanding Radioactivity

# *What is Matter?*

The continual subdivision of a pure substance or element, such as copper, presents two possibilities. One is that you can continually subdivide until eternity and you keep getting the same substance, in other words that matter is continuous. The alternative notion, that you eventually arrive at a piece that if subdivided no longer maintains the properties of the original material, has its origins in early Greece. The philosopher Leucippus (450-370 BC) is credited with the idea that matter is composed of small indivisible particles. This atomic idea was further developed by the laughing philosopher Democritus (460-370 BC). The Greek word 'atomos' means indivisible.

The first scientific evidence for the atomic theory is much more recent and the credit goes to John Dalton (1766-1844), who discovered that compound substances were always formed from 'definite proportions' of elementary substances. In water, which is a compound of oxygen and hydrogen, the mass of oxygen is always eight times that of hydrogen. We now accept that an oxygen atom is 16 times heavier than a hydrogen atom and thus the basic combination of atoms in water is two hydrogens for every oxygen atom, giving $H_2O$.

By the end of the last and the early part of this century scientists realised that the atom was not indivisible and that there are sub-atomic particles known as the proton, the neutron and the electron. A simple picture of the atom suffices for most people, although for a fuller picture of its complexities one must delve into the realm and mysteries of quantum mechanics. The simpler working model of the atom is the solar system idea, proposed by the great New Zealand experimental physicist Lord Ernest Rutherford (1871-1937). His model is that of negatively charged *electrons* of negligible mass, orbiting around a central positive *nucleus* that contains the mass of the atom in its *protons* and *neutrons*. The overall atom is usually uncharged, as the number of negative electrons is balanced by an equal number of oppositely charged protons. Neutrons have no charge, but are of almost similar mass as the protons.

It is important to realise that it is the number of protons in the nucleus that makes one atom different to another. An atom with one proton is hydrogen (H), while one with 2 is always helium (He), and one with 92 is always uranium (U), irrespective of the number of neutrons or electrons. This number is called the atomic number

(Z) of the atom, while the sum of the number of protons and neutrons is called the atomic mass number (A).

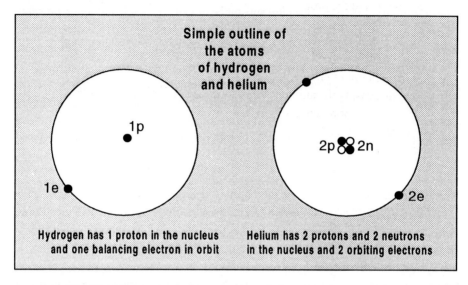

**Simple outline of the atoms of hydrogen and helium**

Hydrogen has 1 proton in the nucleus and one balancing electron in orbit     Helium has 2 protons and 2 neutrons in the nucleus and 2 orbiting electrons

An atom like H with its one proton can have 0, 1 or 2 neutrons making possible three different types of hydrogen atoms called hydrogen isotopes. These are called hydrogen (H-1), deuterium (H-2) and tritium (H-3) with atomic masses of 1, 2 and 3 respectively. Atoms are often written as follows: $_Z X^A$ where X is the symbol for the particular atom, for example, $_1 H^1$ for hydrogen, $_1 H^2$ for deuterium and $_1 H^3$ is tritium.

Uranium also has isotopes, the two most important being U-235 and U-238. This means that while U isotopes always have 92 protons the former has 143 neutrons and the latter has 146 neutrons. It is these isotopes that provide the fuel for electricity generating nuclear power plants.

## Ionisation

Electrons exist in orbits, spinning around the nucleus as the planets rotate around the sun. If they weren't spinning they would collapse into the positively charged nucleus, as unlike charges attract each other (as do the opposite poles of a magnet). The further the electrons are from the nucleus the less strongly they are attracted and thus the easier it is to detach them from the atom. It still requires a kick of energy to knock them from the atom.

If you knocked off one electron the remaining atom would now have a charge of +1 as there would be an excess of one positively charged proton. Such an atom is called an *ion* and the process of creating an ion is called *ionisation*.

One buys coal by the ton and cocaine by the gram. We use units of measurement appropriate to the dimensions of the thing in question. So because atoms are so tiny and the amount of energy to cause an ion is very small a special small unit is used when discussing the amount of energy needed to cause ionisation. It is called the *electron volt*, abbreviated to eV. It takes about 13 eV to knock the electron off a hydrogen atom and make a hydrogen ion. If you wanted to create a million hydrogen ions you would need one million bits of energy each of 13 eV in size. You would need 13,000,000 eV or 13 MeV where M means mega for a million.

## Radioactivity

Although the nucleus contains the mass of the atom it is very small in volume compared with the size of the atom. This means the positive protons are so closely squashed together that they should be repelling each other by electrostatic repulsion and shooting out of the nucleus and indeed the atom. In other words atoms should be unstable and continually breaking up. This is usually not the case in nature otherwise substances would be continually changing into other substances.

There must exist a stronger force, that can overcome this electrostatic repulsion. It is given the descriptive title of the *strong nuclear force* and its strength seems to depend on the ratio of protons and neutrons. Too many - or too few - neutrons relative to the number of protons and the force gets sufficiently weak for the nucleus to fire out some of its constituents (as *alpha* or *beta* particles) until it re-establishes the balance of protons and neutrons back into a stable ratio. This process of nuclei firing out alpha or beta particles is called radioactivity.

An alpha particle is the same as a helium nucleus containing two protons and two neutrons, while the most common beta particle is the same as an electron. When this happens the emitting atom *transmutes* into a new substance, because it will have a new atomic number (number of protons). Radium gives out an alpha ($\alpha$) to become the now familiar radon gas. Carbon-14, which is used for archaeological dating, gives out a beta ($\beta$) particle to become ordinary nitrogen.

How often a particle is ejected from a radioactive isotope is a measure of its *activity* and it can be counted as the number of emissions or decays per second. If an element shoots out one particle or ray a second we say it has an activity of 1 Becquerel (Bq) in honour of the scientist who discovered radioactivity.

In the US they still use a much bigger unit of activity in honour of the Curies, which is the activity one would get from one gram of radium, an element which Marie Curie isolated. This amount of activity is called one Curie (Ci) and it equals 37 billion decays per second or $3.7.10^{10}$ Bq.

Things fall down to the earth rather than up in the air. To get them back up to where they were, before they fell, would require an input of energy or effort. It is a well known fact of nature that all matter seeks the lowest possible energy position that is available to it. When an unstable atom shoots out a radioactive particle its nucleus is usually left in a high energy state. It can lower this value by losing or emitting energy. It does so in the form of a wavelike chunk of radiation called a *photon*. This wave is a bundle of high frequency electromagnetic radiation called a gamma ray. Gamma ($\gamma$) radiation is very similar to x-rays.

## Interacting with matter

When one talks about radioactivity $\alpha$, $\beta$ and $\gamma$ are the three radiation types usually referred to. In a nuclear reactor, one encounters a fourth type of radiation, that of neutrons, because, as we have discussed in the relevant section, it is neutrons that make nuclear reactions possible. We can think of these radiations as atomic bullets carrying energy in the MeV range.

What happens when they encounter or bang into matter in the form of other atoms? Imagine a saucer with some light steel nails on it. If a magnet is dragged close by the saucer you would expect some of the nails to be ripped from the saucer or at least some of the nails will be disturbed or *excited*. A charged radio-active particle such as an alpha (the magnet) has the same effect on the electrons of an atom (the nails) when it passes by.

Electrons can be stripped off the atom, causing the atoms to be *ionised*, or sometimes the electrons might be lifted to a higher energy state without ionisation taking place. Because alpha particles have two charges they have greater ionising power than beta with their single charge. Gamma rays (and also neutrons) have no charge and do not interact with matter by attracting or pulling off electrons. Instead they behave like atomic bullets, by colliding with atoms and often knocking off electrons and thus causing ionisation.

Alpha rays are more ionising than betas, which in turn are more ionising than gamma rays: $\alpha > \beta > \gamma$.

It takes energy to cause ionisation. If a runaway lorry entered a carpark it would collide with a number of vehicles and eventually lose its energy and come to a stop. It is the same with radiation. As radiation creates ions on its journey through matter it will eventually run out of steam and stop. We have seen that it takes about 13 eV to ionise a hydrogen atom. It takes about 30 eV to ionise molecules of oxygen and nitrogen in the air. This means that a typical ray with energy of $3.10^6$ eV (3 MeV) could cause 100,000 ($1.10^5$) ions before losing all its energy.

Because alphas are highly ionising they lose their energy very quickly and therefore they only travel a few centimetres in air and a few micrometers in tissue. They can be blocked by paper. Betas penetrate much further while gammas, with a low ionising power, travel large distances. To block gamma radiation one needs a dense material like lead if space is limited as in a laboratory. In a nuclear power station where space is not a problem, big amounts of less dense materials, such as concrete or water can be used. The powers of penetration are opposite to the abilities of the radiations to ionise: $\alpha < \beta < \gamma$.

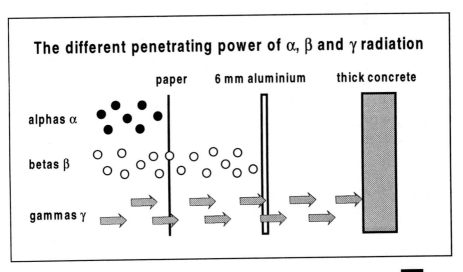

**The different penetrating power of $\alpha$, $\beta$ and $\gamma$ radiation**

paper     6 mm aluminium     thick concrete

alphas $\alpha$

betas $\beta$

gammas $\gamma$

## Carbon dating

How active is a radioactive element (how many decays does it undergo in a second)? This depends on how much of the radioactive isotope is present and on the particular material itself. Radioactive decay is a random process, meaning one cannot predict when a particular atom will disintegrate. This also means that if one has a quantity of a radioactive isotope it may never totally disappear and therefore it would not make sense to talk about the full life of the isotope. For that reason scientists refer to the length of time it takes for half of the radioactive material to decay, its *half life*. U-238 has a half life of about 5 billion years. This is about the age of the earth which means about half of the original uranium at the creation still remains. C-14 has a half life of about 5,700 years while 50% of radon decays in just under 4 days. Some elements exist for only fractions of seconds. The slower the rate of decay the longer the half life.

Most people are familiar with the idea of exponential population growth rates which means that the population of humans or bugs in a culture will double in some set time. Radioactive isotopes decay exponentially. Fifty percent of the C-14 atoms in an ancient remnant of a tree trunk from say the Ceide Fields in Mayo will remain after 5,700 years and 25% will remain after another half life - 11,400 years. Thus as one knows the ratio of C-14 to non-radioactive C-12 in the tree the age of the specimen can be calculated to a high degree of accuracy by using a graph of the exponential decay of the C-14.

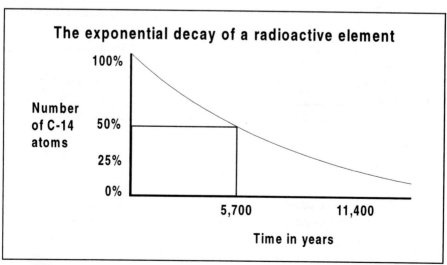

The exponential decay of a radioactive element

We have seen that the emission of a radioactive particle ($\alpha$ and $\beta$ but not $\gamma$ ray) changes or transmutes the element into a new element by changing the number of protons. With the heavier elements, such as uranium-235, uranium-238 and thorium-232, radioactive decay produces other radioactive elements where the strong nuclear force is still not sufficient to keep the new nucleus intact. Therefore further decays and resultant transmutations take place until a stable element is produced. Such a chain of decays produces what is called a radioactive series.

There are four very important such series in nature, one of which begins with U-238 and produces radium and radon along the series. One can follow the transformations in this series and why the atomic (proton) numbers and masses (protons + neutrons) are as shown. Half lives are included. Radioactive isotopes referred to in the text are shown in black boxes.

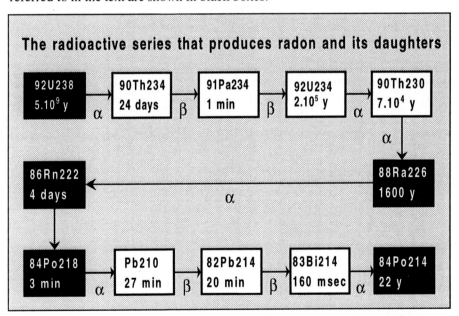

**The radioactive series that produces radon and its daughters**

| 92U238 | 90Th234 | 91Pa234 | 92U234 | 90Th230 |
|---|---|---|---|---|
| $5.10^9$ y | 24 days | 1 min | $2.10^5$ y | $7.10^4$ y |

$\alpha$    $\beta$    $\beta$    $\alpha$

$\alpha$

| 86Rn222 | | | | 88Ra226 |
|---|---|---|---|---|
| 4 days | | $\alpha$ | | 1600 y |

| 84Po218 | Pb210 | 82Pb214 | 83Bi214 | 84Po214 |
|---|---|---|---|---|
| 3 min | 27 min | 20 min | 160 msec | 22 y |

$\alpha$    $\beta$    $\beta$    $\alpha$

## Geiger counters

Just as many forms of radiation are not detectable by the human senses so it is with radioactivity. We use special detectors for measurement. One of the main methods is to use the ionising power of the radiations. As ions are electrical they can be collected to produce a spurt of charge called a pulse. The detectors can count these pulses and thus tell the activity of the source. Not only this but one can obtain instruments that can also measure the energy of the radioactive rays. This is easily done because the greater the energy of the ray the more ions it can cause and therefore the bigger the electric pulse it can create.

The best known detector is the Geiger Counter, called after one of Rutherford's students. It is just a counter of the activity but cannot measure the energy. It is cheap and good for telling you if there is radioactivity in an environment such as the beaches near Sellafield. It cannot, however, tell you what the radioactive isotopes are. To do this you need to be able to measure the energy of the radiations.

The reason for this is that elements emit rays of characteristic fingerprint energies. Alpha rays emitted by radon-222 always has an energy of 5.5 MeV while that of plutonium-239 is always 5.2 MeV. The gamma ray emitted by caesium-137 is always 660 keV while that of radium-226 is 186 keV. This means that if you can measure the energy of the ray, and you can, then you can identify the element that produces it. Such an instrument is called a spectrometer. Therefore, if people in Dundalk or in Berkshire wished to see if there was contamination, due to Sellafield or Greenham Common, then this is possible with modern instrumentation.

Radiographers, workers in the nuclear industry and radiation workers in general wear a film badge as a dosemeter to record their doses. The International Commission on Radiological Protection (ICRP) recommends that all doses should be kept **as low as is reasonably achievable** (the ALARA principle). Therefore the continuous monitoring of radiation workers is the norm.

## Radiation doses

We have seen that ionising radiation, be it particulate as in alpha and beta, or electromagnetic, like X and gamma radiation, carries sufficient energy to create ionisation in matter, including in human tissue. Furthermore an alpha particle loses its energy very quickly creating a huge amount of ionisation in a very small volume of tissue. Ionising radiation deposits energy and the amount of energy deposited in a given quantity of tissue is called the *dose*.

Already we have seen a tiny unit of energy called the electron volt. In the macroscopic world of cars, footballers and bags of sugar energy is measured in units of *Joules* (J). How much energy would it take to lift a 1 kg bag of sugar from the floor onto a table? It would take about 10 J. One joule is more than a billion billion times ($10^{18}$) the size of an eV and a thousand billion ($10^{12}$) times the size of 1 MeV.

Given that ionising radiation typically carries about one MeV of energy you would need about a thousand billion rays to deposit one joule of energy. This may seem enormous but elements vary in their activity. We saw that 1 gram (g) of radium gives a Curie or about ten billion decays per second ($3.7.10^{10}$ Bq) of radioactivity. 1 g of radium could deliver a joule of energy in a couple of minutes.

Henri Becquerel, not knowing the health risks of radiation used to carry around some radium, a present from his friends the Curies, in his pocket until he found his skin suffering radiation burns. Burning tissue requires energy.

It may seem amazing that such a small quantity of an element could have so many atoms decaying every second. One must remember that atoms are very small and 1 g of Ra contain about a thousand billion billion billion or $10^{21}$ atoms. If the activity is about $10^{10}$ Bq then only one hundredth billion ($10^{-11}$) of the atoms are decaying in any second. 50% of this radium will still be there after one half life in 1,600 years, so this rate of decay is fairly slow.

The basic definition of radiation absorbed dose is the amount of energy absorbed by a one kilogram mass of material. If the amount of energy is 1 J (remember your bag of sugar) then this is called 1 gray (Gy) of absorbed dose. The older unit, still used in the US is the rad. One gray is a dose of 1 J per kg.

But we have already seen that different radiations can cause different degrees of harm to the human body.

Alpha is considered 20 times more harmful than gamma, so for this reason we need to give the different radiations 'weightings'. When we multiply the absorbed dose in grays by the weighting we get another unit called the *sievert* (Sv).

*1 Gy of alpha radiation = 20 Sv while 1 Gy of gamma = 1 Sv*

This unit is called the 'absorbed dose equivalent' as we have now made all the radiations equivalent for potential to do harm. 1 Gy of alpha radiation will carry the same risk of damage to the lung or testes as 20 Gy of gamma radiation.

The picture is further complicated because the risk of a fatal effect from a given dose equivalent of radiation is not the same for the various tissues in the body. The risk is much lower for the thyroid than the lung or the ovaries. Various tissues are assigned a weighting factor to account for their different susceptibilities to radiation risk.

If the whole body is assigned a risk factor of 1 then the various tissues and organs have values as follows:

| testes and ovaries | 0.25 | liver | 0.06 |
|---|---|---|---|
| breast | 0.15 | thyroid | 0.03 |
| red bone marrow | 0.12 | bone surface | 0.03 |
| lung | 0.12 | rest of body | 0.24 |

This is useful for radiation health scientists or radiologists because they can now compare the doses to the various tissues in terms of a whole body dose. For example a dose of 400 mSv to the ovaries would have the same effect as a whole body dose of 100 mSv. A dose of 3,300 mSv to the thyroid is also equivalent to a whole body dose of 100 mSv and therefore carries with it the same risk of fatal malignancy as the previous dose to the ovaries.

## More about alpha and beta particles

If a nucleus has too many neutrons it can emit a beta particle, which is like an electron, except it comes from the nucleus which contains no negative particles. Therefore it must come from a transformation of a proton or a neutron. If there is an excess of neutrons then the elimination of a neutron will be good for the stability of the nucleus and thus a neutron changes into a proton. But in order to balance the electrical charges it changes into a proton and an electron-like beta particle. The latter is shot out of the nucleus like a bullet, with energy in the MeV range.

*Radiation level sampling*

$$_0n^1 \longrightarrow {_1}p^1 + {_{-1}}\beta^0$$

This is what happens in the case of carbon 14 ( $_6C^{14}$ ) the radioactive element used in radioactive dating of archaeological artefacts. The normal carbon that constitutes most of the carbon in the world, as in coal or carbon dioxide in the atmosphere - is $_6C^{12}$ - having an equal number of protons and neutrons. C-14 with its excess of neutrons is unstable, having a strong nuclear force that is not strong enough to keep the nucleus permanently intact. One neutron transforms into a proton and a negative beta particle, giving us a new nucleus with 7 protons and 7 neutrons, which is, of course, no longer carbon but nitrogen. This is an example of a radioactive disintegration or decay:

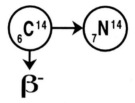

An important example of beta emission happens in a nuclear reactor where the element U-238 can absorb neutrons which are readily available in reactors and become the more unstable isotope U-239, with a real excess of neutrons. It changes (via neptunium) into the very radiotoxic and dangerous substance plutonium 239 after two beta decays. Plutonium is an artificial element with a higher atomic number than uranium and is thus called a transuranic element. Transuranic elements are produced in the fabrication of nuclear weapons and to a lesser extent in the generation of electricity by nuclear power:

$$_{92}U^{239} \longrightarrow {_{93}}Np^{239} + \beta^- \quad \text{then} \quad _{93}Np^{239} \longrightarrow {_{94}}Pu^{239} + \beta^-$$

Alpha particles are similar to helium atoms with the two electrons removed or in other words they are helium nuclei. It is usually the heavier elements that emit alphas when they are unstable. Well known examples are U-235, Ra-226 and the topical radon, Rn-222:

$$_{86}Ra^{226} \longrightarrow {_{84}}Rn^{222} + {_2}\alpha^4$$

In all these events or reactions the atomic (or charge) number and the mass number is conserved, so that nothing is being created or destroyed, which is a fundamental principle in science.

The ionising and penetrating powers have major implications for the protection of people from ionising radiation, especially people who work in radiation occupations such as radio-therapists in hospitals or in nuclear industries or research. Alpha radiation, if external, will not penetrate the outer skin of the body and is therefore relatively safe while gamma and obviously X-rays are highly penetrating and thus must be shielded against. Alternatively, internal alpha sources are highly hazardous as they deposit all their energy in a small volume of tissue. Hence the present radon scare as radon is an alpha emitter. Internal sources of gamma radiation are quite likely to escape from the body and are less dangerous.

Two of the main sources of evidence for the damage that radioactivity can cause come from the study of Japanese people after the atomic bombs of the second world war and the deaths from lung cancer of uranium miners in many parts of the world. The former suffered from acute high doses of external gamma radiation, while the latter were victims of the chronic exposure to internal alpha doses from inhaled radon.

## *Appendix i*

This appendix lists all the elements referred to in the text, gives their scientific symbols and shows whether they are alpha or beta emitters. Almost all radioactive elements give out gamma radiation in conjunction with the other two.

# Symbols of elements

| | | | | | |
|---|---|---|---|---|---|
| americium | Am | $\alpha$ | barium | Ba | |
| bismuth | Bi | $\alpha$ | carbon | C-14 | $\beta$ |
| cobalt | Co | $\beta$ | helium | He | |
| hydrogen | H | | iodine | I | $\beta$ |
| krypton | Kr | $\beta$ | lead | Pb | |
| nitrogen | N | | oxygen | O | |
| palladium | Pa | $\alpha$ | plutonium | Pu | $\alpha$ |
| polonium | Po | $\alpha$ | potassium | K-40 | $\beta$ |
| radium | Ra | $\alpha$ | radon | Rn | $\alpha$ |
| strontium | Sr | $\beta$ | technetium | Tc | $\beta$ |
| thorium | Th | $\beta$ | tritium | H-3 | $\beta$ |
| uranium | U | $\alpha$ | | | |

## *Appendix ii*

## Glossary of units

| | |
|---|---|
| **Amps** | The unit of electric current: A |
| **Becquerel** | How active a radionuclide is, in decays per second: Bq |
| **Electron Volt** | A very small unit of energy: $1J \approx 10^{19}$ eV |
| **Gray** | Radiation absorbed dose in joules per kilogram: Gy |
| **Joules** | The unit of energy: J |
| **MeV** | A million electron volts: $1$ MeV $= 10^6$ eV |
| **Sievert** | Absorbed dose equivalent. Allows for different damage by $\alpha$, $\beta$ and $\gamma$ radiations |
| **Volt** | The unit of voltage: V |
| **Watts** | Unit of power or the number of joules per second: 1 Watt = 1J/s |
| **Watts/sq. metre** | Power density. The energy passing through an area per second: $W/m^2$ |
| **Watts/kilogram** | Energy absorbed by unit mass per second: W/kg |

## Acronyms

| | |
|---|---|
| **ALARA** | As low as reasonably achievable |
| **ANSI** | American National Standards Institute |
| **EMF** | Electromagnetic frequency radiation |
| **ELF** | Extremely low frequency radiation (50/60 Hz) |
| **EPA** | Environmental Protection Agency |
| **ICRP** | International Commission for Radiological Protection |
| **ICNIRP** | International Commission on Non-Ionising Radiation Protection |
| **IRPA** | International Radiation Protection Association |
| **MMDS** | Multipoint Microwave Distribution System |
| **NIR** | Non-ionising radiation |
| **NRPB** | National Radiation Protection Board in the UK |
| **RF** | Radiofrequencies |
| **RPII** | Radiological Protection Institute of Ireland |
| **SAR** | Specific Absorption Rate |

## *Appendix iii*

## Basic Reference Glossary

**Terms in the text that are written in italics, when first met, are briefly defined in this basic reference glossary.**
**A greater understanding of most of them can be obtained by working through Section C, *Understanding Radiation.***

**activity**
The number of radioactive emissions in a second.
Measured in units of Becquerels (Bq).
1 Bq is 1 radioactive emission or decay per second.

**acute**
Refers to a dose that is received in a short time period.

**alpha (α)**
A radioactive particle that is emitted from certain radioactive elements such as radon.
It is a helium nucleus containing 2 protons and 2 neutrons.

**amps (A)**
The unit of electric current. Domestic fuses are rated in amps, for example; a 13 A fuse is used in the plug of a kettle or heater.

**atoms**
The smallest individual part of an element, contains protons and neutrons in a central nucleus, with electrons orbiting about this nucleus. The number of protons determines what the element is, while the sum of protons and neutrons determines the mass, or mass number, of the atom. An atom has no nett electrical charge if the number of protons (+ charges) equals the oppositely charged electrons (- charges).
there are no electrons.

**atomic symbols**
There are about 100 elements in existence, of which 92 are natural. Each element has a universally accepted abbreviation, or symbol, which often derives from its Latin name.
The symbol for iron is Fe, from Ferrum. When discussing radioactive atoms, or isotopes, the mass number of the isotope

is written after the symbol. Two important isotopes of uranium (U), used in nuclear power stations, have mass numbers of 235 and 238 and are written U-235 and U-238 respectively. Potassium (K) has two isotopes, K-39 and K-40.

**background**   The level of radiation that normally exists in our environment. It can be natural or man made in origin.

**Becquerels**   (Bq) The unit of radioactivity. 10 Bq means 10 decays every second.

**beta (β)**   A radioactive particle that is emitted from certain radioactive elements, such as carbon-14 or caesium-137. It is similar to an electron, except it comes out of the nucleus where

**chronic**   Refers to a dose that is delivered over a long period of time.

**compound**   Is a substance composed of one or more elements, eg, water is composed of the elements hydrogen and oxygen.

**daughter**   When a radioactive element changes, or transmutes, into another element, the element formed is called a radioactive daughter. Radon-222 is the daughter of radium-226. Ra-226 is called the parent. In a radioactive series one finds many daughters.

**DC and AC**   Refers to the direction that electric current flows in a wire. When one puts an ordinary battery into a torch the current flows in the one direction through the bulb all the time. This is a direct or DC current and the battery would be a DC battery. If the current was constantly pushed in one direction and then in the opposite direction by the battery we would have an AC, or alternating current, caused by an AC battery. The bulb would still light, as the direction of the current through it is irrelevant to its operation. This is what happens in the domestic bulb.

**decay**

Also called disintegration. When a radioactive particle is emitted from a radioactive atom the process is called a decay, because the atom no longer remains the same atom but changes or transmutes into another atom. The time taken for half of the atoms to decay is called the half life of the element.

**disintegration**

See decay, above.

**dose**

Is a measure of the amount of radiation one is exposed to, or that is deposited in our bodies. With radioactive exposure it is a measure of the amount of energy absorbed by the body and is measured in units of grays or sieverts. It is more difficult to quantify dose with non-ionising radiations, like microwaves, but a common measure is the amount of energy per second, or watts per kilogram of tissue.

**electromagnetic spectrum**

Is the family of waves that have an electric and magnetic nature and travel at the speed of light. It includes radio waves, microwaves, infra red, visible, ultraviolet and X-radiation. It does not include waves such as sound or waves on water. The energy of these waves depends on their wavelengths or frequencies and is very high for X-rays and low for radio waves.

**electrons (e)**

Tiny, almost massless, negative charges that circle about the nucleus of an atom. They are what allow atoms to join together to make molecules.

**electron volt (eV)**

A tiny unit of energy used when describing the energy carried by electrons or radioactive rays. The latter usually carry about a million electron volts and the symbol M is often used to describe a million or mega electron volts (MeV).

**elements**

Substances which contain only one type of atom and cannot be subdivided into other substances, eg, iron, uranium and hydrogen.

**epidemiology**

The statistical study of the relationship between disease and various factors, such as radon or non ionising radiation, in a population. The existence of a statistical relationship does not necessarily imply a causal connection.

**excited**

When energy is added to an atom its electrons gain energy and are moved further away from the nucleus. If this energy is not enough to remove the electron from the atom (ionisation) we say the atom is in an excited state. The nucleus is often left in an excited state after an alpha or beta particle has been ejected from it.

**fallout**

The radioactive material that falls out of the atmosphere after a nuclear explosion or emission.

**fast breeder reactor**

A nuclear reactor that uses plutonium as a fuel, but in doing so is capable of turning or transmuting uranium-238 surrounding the fuel into more plutonium than the reaction uses up. It could thus provide more fuel than it uses up. There is no commercial FBR in operation for the generation of electricity.

**fields**

Are regions of space where forces of certain types can be experienced. We are most familiar with gravitational fields, as we constantly live in one. In a gravitational field an object must have mass to experience a gravitational force. An electric field will exert a force on a charged particle, such as an electron or a proton. A magnetic field will exert a force on anything having a magnetic nature. As moving charged particles, such as electrons orbiting the atom, behave as magnets, the atoms in our bodies can experience forces due to magnetic fields.

**fission**
The splitting of an atom. In a nuclear reactor this usually happens when uranium-235 or plutonium-239 are bombarded with slow moving neutrons. A lot of energy is released when this happens. Einstein's famous equation $E = mc^2$ is used to calculate the amount of energy produced.

**frequency**
The number of times something happens, or the number of vibrations in a second. 1 vibration a second is called 1 hertz (Hz). The frequency of the musical note 'middle C' is 256 Hz, while to tune into 98FM radio in Dublin one must tune a radio receiver to the 98 kilohertz (98 kHz) frequency mark.

**gamma (γ)**
A highly penetrating form of electromagnetic radiation that is emitted from the nucleus of a radioactive element. It is similar to X-radiation. The radioactive emission of an alpha or beta particle changes the composition of the nucleus and thus changes the element into a new element. The emission of a gamma ray has no effect on the composition of the nucleus.

**genetic**
A genetic effect of radiation has health consequences for the offspring of the exposed individual.

**giga (G)**
A prefix that multiplies a unit by a billion ($10^9$). Microwaves have frequencies in the GHz range.

**gray (Gy)**
The unit of absorbed dose from radioactive exposure. It is a measure of energy absorbed by a kilogram of matter, organ or tissue. 1 gray (1 Gy) is one joule of energy per kilogram (1 J/kg).

**half-life**
The length of time it takes half the amount of a radioactive element to decay. For radon-222 it is almost 4 days. If one had a jar containing 1,000 radon atoms there would only be 500 remaining after 4 days and only 250 after 8 days. The greater the activity of a radioactive element the shorter the half life and vice versa.

**hertz (Hz)**     Is the unit of frequency, the number of vibrations per second.

**hot spot**     A place where exposure to radiation is unusually high.

**ions**     These are atoms that have had electrons removed or added. If a negatively charged electron is knocked off an atom then the atom has an extra proton (+ charge) becoming an atom with one + charge. A charged atom is called an ion. If an electron is added to the atom it becomes a negatively charged ion.
An alpha particle which has two protons and no electrons is an ion with two positive charges (+2).

**ionisation**     The process by which an ion is formed. Radioactive rays cause ionisation, by pulling electrons off an atom, which is why they are dangerous. Energy is needed to cause an ion. It takes about 30 eV of energy to ionise an air molecule. Therefore 30 MeV could ionise one million air molecules.

**ionising**     This applies to all radiations (electromagnetic and radioactive)
**radiation**     that possess sufficient energy to knock electrons off atoms and thus cause ions.

**intensity**     As a beam of light or radiation spreads out with distance from the source of the radiation it gets weaker. The radiation energy in the beam is spread out over a larger area. There is less radiation energy and power per area ($W/m^2$).

**isotope**     Atoms of the same element can often have different numbers of neutrons in their nuclei. This causes the atoms to have different masses or mass numbers. These atoms are called isotopes. Potassium (K) usually has a mass number of 39 (19 protons + 20 neutrons) but a small fraction (0.01%) of potassium atoms in nature are slightly heavier with a mass number of 40 (19 protons + 21 neutrons). This gives 2 isotopes of potassium, K-39 and radioactive K-40.

**joule (J)**  This is the normal scientific unit of energy. One unit of ESB electricity which costs about 8 pence contains 3.6 million joules (3.6.10$^6$ J) of energy. This is enough energy to keep a 100 watt (100 J/s) electric bulb lit for 10 hours. Because each radioactive ray carries only a small amount of energy a smaller unit of energy is used when stating the energy of the ray. This unit is called the electron volt.

**latency period**  There are many years between the initiation of a cancer and the appearance of its symptoms.

**leachate**  The soluble material that is extracted from solid waste by rainwater and flows into streams or ground water.

**lethal dose**  Lethal Dose $_{30,50}$ This is the dose that will kill 50% of a population in 30 days.

**line of sight**  Is when a straight line can be drawn between two objects. Mobile phone microwaves travel in straight lines and thus antennae must be able to 'see' each other.

**linear assumption**  At high radiation doses there is a high risk of resultant health effects. It is not possible to say what the effects are for low doses, so the ICRP assume a straight line relationship between dose and effect.

**mass number**  The mass of the nucleus of an atom. It is the sum of the number of protons and neutrons in the nucleus.

**mega**  A prefix for a unit that multiplies that unit by a million (10$^6$). Mobile phones operate at a frequency of 900 MHz. Radioactive particles have energies of the order of 1 to 5 MeV.

**MeV**  Mega or a million (10$^6$) electron volts. Radioactive rays usually carry energies in the MeV range. It would take about a million million (10$^{12}$) MeV to make one joule of energy.

**micro (m)**  A prefix for a unit that divides that unit by a million ($10^6$). One micrometre (1 μm) is a million times smaller than a metre (m) and a thousand ($10^3$) times smaller than a millimetre (mm).

**milli (m)**  A prefix for a unit that divides that unit by a thousand ($10^3$). One milli sievert (mSv) is a thousand times smaller than a sievert (Sv) and a thousand times greater than a micro sievert (μSv).

**molecules**  When atoms combine they are called molecules. Atoms are the smallest part of an element that is still the element while molecules are the smallest characteristic part of a compound. A water molecule is composed of one oxygen atom and two hydrogen atoms and the molecule is symbolically written as $H_2O$.

**nano (n)**  Prefix that divides a unit by a billion ($10^9$). The wavelengths of the electromagnetic spectrum that the human eye is sensitive to range from 400 nm for violet light to 700 nm for red light.

**nucleus**  It is the centre of the atom, in the same way as the sun is the centre of the solar system. It contains the mass of the atom in its protons and neutrons. The sum of these gives the mass number of the atom. All radioactive processes are nuclear, meaning they have their origin in the nucleus. So if the nucleus emits an alpha particle its mass number is going to be smaller by the mass number of the alpha particle (which is 4). So when radon-222 decays by emitting an alpha-4 particle we get a new atom which has a mass number of 218. This is also a new element, called polonium-218.

**neutrons (n)**  These are neutral particles, of equal mass with the protons, which, along with protons, constitute the nucleus of an atom. In atoms where the number of protons remain the same but the number of neutrons vary one gets isotopes. Uranium-235 contains 143 neutrons while U-238 contains 146 neutrons.

**parent**     See daughter above.

**pathway**     The routes through the food chain by which toxic materials can reach what we ingest or inhale.

**photon**     Although waves of radiation do not have any mass or weight we can imagine them behaving like bullets or bundles of energy when they interact or collide with matter. These bundles are called photons and their energy depends on their frequency.

**power**     Is the rate of using energy. This is the number of joules of energy used per second. It is measured in watts (W). A 100 W bulb uses 100 joules of energy per second.

**power density**     Radiation carries energy. Imagine the beam of a torch (or a radar transmitter) falling on a wall. The more of the beam you can concentrate onto a smaller area the more intense it will become. There is more energy per second falling onto this area (per area). The power density has been increased. It is measured in joules per second per area which means the same as watts per area. The area is usually expressed as squared metres or as squared centimetres.

**protons (p)**     Constituents of the nucleus along with neutrons. They are positively charged particles. Their number determines what the element is. An atom with one proton is always hydrogen, irrespective of the number of neutrons or electrons in the atom. An atom with 92 protons is always uranium.

**radioactive decay series**     A radioactive series is when one element transmutes or changes into another element, which in turn transmutes into another and so on, until a non radioactive element is formed. Radon-222 belongs to the radioactive series that begins with uranium-238.

**SAR**     The specific absorption rate. Is a measure of the amount of non ionising radiation energy absorbed by a kilogram of matter, or tissue, in a second. It is measured in joules per kilogram per second, which is the same as watts per kilogram (W/kg).

**sievert**    A refinement of the gray, which is the unit of radiation absorbed dose. It takes into account the fact that alpha radiation can cause more biological damage than beta and gamma radiation, because it has greater ionising power than the other radiations. Grays are turned into sieverts by multiplying by a factor from 1 to 20, depending on the type of radiation. The factor is 1 for gamma radiation, so 1 Gy of gamma is equivalent to 1 Sv, while 1 Gy of alpha radiation is equivalent to 20 Sv, since the factor for alpha is 20.

**somatic**    A somatic effect of radiation exposure involves health consequences for the exposed individual.

**stochastic**    A stochastic effect is a random effect. Radiation induced
**(and**    cancer is an example, as one cannot predict who will be
**deterministic)**    affected. The greater the dose the greater the chance, or probability, of an individual suffering an effect. In non-stochastic (or deterministic) effects the severity of the effect of the exposure will depend on the size of the dose. Non-stochastic radiation effects are those where there is a definite threshold dose, below which the effect will not occur.

**strong**    Because the nucleus is full of positively charged protons one
**nuclear force**    would expect them to repel each other and thus break up the nucleus. As this seldom happens there must be a force stronger than this electric repulsive force of the protons. It is called the strong nuclear force. Sometimes it is not strong enough to keep a nucleus intact and then the atom becomes radioactive and kicks out part of the nucleus as alpha or beta particles.

**tera (T)**    A prefix that multiplies a unit by a million times a million ($10^{12}$). Many of the allowed releases from Sellafield are in the range of Tera Becquerel (TBq).

**transmutation**    The changing of an element into a different element. This always happens when an alpha or a beta particle is emitted from the nucleus, because it changes the number of characteristic protons in the nucleus.

**transuranic**     Uranium is the heaviest naturally occurring radioactive element, with 92 protons in its nucleus. Elements with higher numbers of protons, such as plutonium with 94 protons and americium with 95 protons, are man made. Plutonium, which is highly radiotoxic, is a major product in the generation of electricity from uranium 235 in nuclear reactors. Transuranic wastes are highly radiotoxic alpha emitters.

**units**     All quantities are measured in units. Distance is measured in miles, kilometres, light years, millimetres, etc. The choice of unit is often determined by the size of the quantity. It is more convenient to measure the distances of the stars in light years, rather than in millimetres, although it could be stated in millimetres. Similarly, the energy of radioactive particles could be measures in joules (J), but it is more convenient to use the smaller unit of the electron volt (eV) or indeed the MeV.

**volts**     One can think of voltage as that which pushes current through a conductor, like a wire, or the element of a kettle. The greater the voltage the greater the amount of current that will pass through the conductor, assuming the conductor does not melt with the heat. The voltage of a battery for a transistor radio is usually 6 V DC, while the voltage from the ESB in homes is about 220 V AC.

**wavelength**     Is the distance between one crest and the following crest of a wave. Sea waves can be measured in metres, microwaves in millimetres and UV waves in nanometres (nm).

**watts**     Is the unit of power. Power is the speed that energy can be used or delivered. A 10 horsepower car has a power of about 7,500 watts (W). This provides 7,500 joules of energy per second (J/s).

**W/cm2**     A unit of power density.
          See power density above.